I0407972

Editor-in-Chief and Founder:
  Lyndon H. LaRouche, Jr.
Editorial Board: *Lyndon H. LaRouche, Jr. , Helga Zepp-LaRouche, Robert Ingraham, Tony Papert, Gerald Rose, Dennis Small, Jeffrey Steinberg, William Wertz*
Co-Editors: *Robert Ingraham, Tony Papert*
Managing Editor: *Nancy Spannaus*
Technology: *Marsha Freeman*
Books: *Katherine Notley*
Ebooks: *Richard Burden*
Graphics: *Alan Yue*
Photos: *Stuart Lewis*
Circulation Manager: *Stanley Ezrol*

INTELLIGENCE DIRECTORS
Counterintelligence: *Jeffrey Steinberg, Michele Steinberg*
Economics: *John Hoefle, Marcia Merry Baker, Paul Gallagher*
History: *Anton Chaitkin*
Ibero-America: *Dennis Small*
Russia and Eastern Europe: *Rachel Douglas*
United States: *Debra Freeman*

INTERNATIONAL BUREAUS
Bogotá: *Miriam Redondo*
Berlin: *Rainer Apel*
Copenhagen: *Tom Gillesberg*
Houston: *Harley Schlanger*
Lima: *Sara Madueño*
Melbourne: *Robert Barwick*
Mexico City: *Gerardo Castilleja Chávez*
New Delhi: *Ramtanu Maitra*
Paris: *Christine Bierre*
Stockholm: *Ulf Sandmark*
United Nations, N.Y.C.: *Leni Rubinstein*
Washington, D.C.: *William Jones*
Wiesbaden: *Göran Haglund*

ON THE WEB
e-mail: eirns@larouchepub.com
www.larouchepub.com
www.executiveintelligencereview.com
www.larouchepub.com/eiw
Webmaster: *John Sigerson*
Assistant Webmaster: *George Hollis*
Editor, Arabic-language edition: *Hussein Askary*

EIR (ISSN 0273-6314) *is published weekly (50 issues), by EIR News Service, Inc., P.O. Box 17390, Washington, D.C. 20041-0390. (703) 297-8434*

European Headquarters: E.I.R. GmbH, Postfach Bahnstrasse 9a, D-65205, Wiesbaden, Germany
Tel: 49-611-73650
Homepage: http://www.eir.de
e-mail: info@eir.de
Director: Georg Neudecker

Montreal, Canada: 514-461-1557
eir@eircanada.ca

Denmark: EIR - Danmark, Sankt Knuds Vej 11, basement left, DK-1903 Frederiksberg, Denmark.
Tel.: +45 35 43 60 40, Fax: +45 35 43 87 57. e-mail: eirdk@hotmail.com.

Mexico City: EIR, Sor Juana Inés de la Cruz 242-2 Col. Agricultura C.P. 11360 Delegación M. Hidalgo, México D.F.
Tel. (5525) 5318-2301
eirmexico@gmail.com

Development Is the New Name for Peace

EIR Contents

www.larouchepub.com Volume 44, Number 17, April 28, 2017

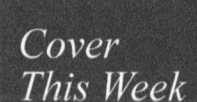

Cover This Week

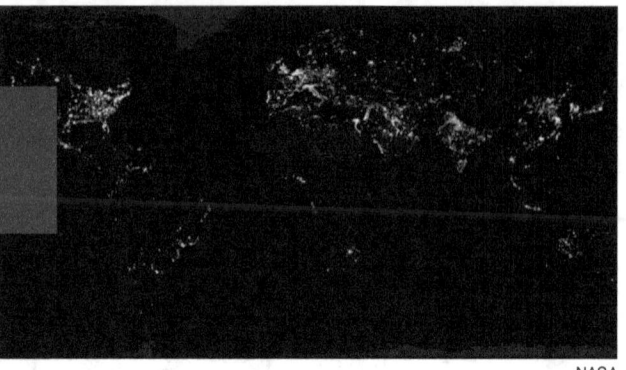

NASA

The Earth at night, seen from space.

The title of this issue is a quotation from Pope Paul VI's Populorum Progressio, *1967.*

I. Britain Goes for War

'You Are Afraid that Russia Might Be Working Together with the United States'

The following is an edited transcript taken from the official, simultaneous voice-over English translation of remarks delivered by Deputy Permanent Representative of the Russian Federation to the United Nations, Vladimir Safronkov, to the UN Security Council on April 12, 2017.

The statement of the representative of Great Britain, Mr. Rycroft, showed that the only thing he's thinking of is to prevent the political process from unfolding, is to bring into the Security Council a confrontational attitude, and the essence is—and everyone in the UN knows this very well—[turning to personally address the British Representative Matthew Rycroft]—that *you are afraid, you are losing sleep over the fact that we might be working together with the United States, cooperating with the United States.* That is what you fear. You are doing everything to make sure that this type of cooperation be undermined. This is precisely why—Look at me when I am speaking! Don't look away! Why are you looking away?—This is precisely why *you* today didn't say anything about the political process. You didn't even listen to Mr. de Mistura's briefing,[1] on purpose. You make insulting demands of the guarantor of the Astana process.[2] What have you done for a ceasefire? You welcomed various opposition groups in London and Paris, illegal armed groups. You suddenly were afraid that things seemed to be moving toward peace and a political solution. Basically, you support the interest of armed groups. Many of them have been murdering Christians and other minorities in the Middle

UN Photo/Manuel Elias

Vladimir K. Safronkov, Deputy Permanent Representative of the Russian Federation to the UN, addresses the Security Council emergency meeting on the situation in Syria.

East. They have been committing terrorist acts in churches on Palm Sunday. That's whose interests you are advancing. What are you doing?

It turns out that regime change for you is more important than the positions of the majority of the member states of the United Nations. Mr. Rycroft, you, today, were speaking not on the topic on our agenda, today. You insulted Syria, Iran, Turkey, other states. Mr. President, I would ask you to make sure that the rules and procedure of this meeting are respected. If some of the members speak insultingly, I cannot accept that you insult Russia. Nevertheless, Mr. de Mistura, we are very grateful to you for your work, and in the run-up to the next round further work will be required to make sure that intra-Syrian dia-

---

1. Staffan de Mistura, special UN envoy to Syria.
2. Syrian peace negotiations, taking place in Astana, Kazakhstan.

logue is truly representative and broad.

The Peace Process

All patriotically motivated Syrian parties should have an opportunity to take part in the negotiations on an equal footing in order to engage in discussions of maintaining Syria as a unified and secular state, where all historical communities would live in peace and take part in rebuilding the country, as has always been the case. From the side of the opposition, there should be an inclusive, consolidated delegation, the members of which should have a common position, bearing in mind the views of the key factions in these delegations. There is no room for arrogance! We need to think not about pride or arrogance, we need to think of the future of Syria. That is the substance of your conceptual document, your note. The idea is to think of the future of their state and for that we shouldn't interfere in their affairs. Let them conduct their dialogue calmly, and please don't interfere with the work of Mr. de Mistura in seeking a formula for a political solution. And I know that, Mr. de Mistura, this is your position. We cannot allow an interruption in the work of state institutions. This applies to security institutions that bear the main burden in combating the terrorist threat. Look at the other countries of the Middle East and Africa and other regions. We can't even greet the state institutions on paper, and what you want is to destroy the ones that are still there in Syria, which is the most important country in the region.

We insist on discussions being held without any preconditions, and we know that that is your position, obviously against the backdrop of political efforts. It is unacceptable that opponents of the government in Damascus have tried to achieve military progress or advances. We recall, on the eve of the previous negotiations, the opposition tried to make an advance in various parts of the front, including near the capital, and we hope that such hot-heads will be condemned and their reckless activity will not be allowed.

This is what we're talking about: You say one thing

AMISOM Public Information

United Kingdom Permanent Representative to the UN Security Council, Matthew Rycroft.

in the Security Council, but you think something else, whereas in fact what you're doing is a third thing. So you think one thing, you say a second thing, and you act a third way. So please, do your work. London and Paris work with various opposition groups. Call them and talk to them and say, "you need to support the Astana process. You cannot fire on the Russian embassy in Damascus."[3] And then you don't agree even to publish an ordinary communiqué, a press release, condemning the attack on the Russian embassy in Damascus, in a situation where tensions have mounted due to the missile strike of the United States.

The importance of the political efforts is becoming more important. Obviously provocations, such as the one that occurred at Khan Sheikhoun,[4] will only strengthen the positions of those who favor a military solution. We need to find out the facts, conduct a comprehensive investigation. I was quite surprised to hear that French experts have already reached the conclusion that Damascus is responsible. I'm amazed that this was the conclusion. No one has yet visited the site of the crime. How do you know that?

The fate of the country should be determined by the Syrians themselves, and not by someone else. That is absolutely clear. We, together with other guarantors, together with Turkey, Iran, and I want to also warmly thank the leadership of Kazakhstan, we are ready to continue working on the Astana platform. Russia is ready to fulfill its obligations in strengthening the cease-fire. But you need to also do your part in working with the various groups, opposition groups. Astana cannot become a panacea in a situation where others are working to undermine it. Significant progress has been made in terms of local truces, which have made it possible to ease the situation and normalize the lives of

---

3. A reference to the Feb. 2 and 3 terrorist attacks on the Russian Embassy in Damascus.

4. The site of the alleged chemical attack, used to justify the subsequent U.S. airstrike.

people from a humanitarian point of view.

Many have said today that the problem of access to besieged areas should be resolved. But let us be fair. Why isn't food supplied to areas that are controlled by the government? Are they just different kinds of people there? Again? Different kinds of people? Let's be honest. We know the situation. We need support from capitals who, for the time being, are just engaged in empty rhetoric and useless criticism. The Astana process has a unique and special value. It is aimed at achieving, in practice, an end to violence, and what's most important is that it is a direct support to the Geneva process, that Mr. de Mistura is leading. We see that Mr. de Mistura and the overwhelming majority of UN member states greatly value the Astana process.

Voice of America/public domain

The International Meeting on Syrian Settlement in Astana, Kazakhstan.

Providing a Future for People

We would like to draw the attention of the international community and the United Nations to significant contamination of the territory of Syria by mines, unexploded ordinance, IEDs, and we regularly inform you of the significant activity by Russian experts to deal with this problem. We call on establishing an international coalition on de-mining Syria. Any kind of blackmail, saying that, "well, we'll de-mine once the regime changes," is unacceptable, it is hypocrisy; it is a completely hypocritical and unacceptable position. I think the specialized UN service could play an important role in this.

Obviously the humanitarian component here is very important. People need to feel safe and secure when they return to their homes, when they return to economic activity, so that children don't explode because of mines, so that civilians don't suffer. We need to clear mines from the world heritage site in Palmyra. These are the kinds of issues that we need to work on. When you discuss the issues of solving the problem of migration, that is what we need to discuss, not regime change, but de-mining, mine clearance, resolving conflicts. People will return to their homes by themselves. They don't need to be forced to do anything. These are the kinds of issues that need to be tackled. We need to work together on improving the social conditions in which people live.

Instead of that, international and regional forums are convened where billions are pledged—virtual billions are pledged!—without even the Syrian representatives being present. How is this related to statements made here in the Security Council that the fate of the Syrian people is in their own hands? Many are seriously thinking about the future, of the post-conflict future of Syria, the return of IDPs [Internally Displaced Persons] and refugees. That would be the most meaningful response to the activity of the terrorists, the most important response. But to exclude Damascus, to exclude the representatives of the Syrian Arab Republic from this process, is unprofessional, unacceptable, unethical, and arrogant.

Political settlement, Mr. de Mistura, is the only way of returning Syria to peace and to easing the tensions in the Middle East.... That is the path toward normalizing the situation in many countries of the Middle East. There is an opportunity of making Syria a model of cooperation for a settlement. But, the very destructive geopolitical projects will not contribute to that. At least, we will not give them a free pass in the Security Council. Thank you very much, Madame President.

Why Is Korea Not Reunified Already?

by Michael Billington

April 22—There is no legitimate reason why Korea has not already been reunified, or why there must now be a festering crisis over North Korea, threatening to spark a war that would devastate most of Asia and could possibly provoke a global nuclear war. The overtly British assets in the White House over the past 16 years—George W. Bush, Dick Cheney, and Barack Obama—intentionally created the crisis, not because of any actions by North Korea, but in order to provoke confrontation or even war between the United States and China, to sustain the British division of the world into East against West. Likewise, we see the desperate effort by the British today to stop President Trump's intended cooperation with Russia—using British-manufactured crises in Ukraine and Syria aimed at maintaining U.S.-Russia antagonism and possible war.

As this article will demonstrate, the foundation for a peaceful resolution to the Korea conflict—including ending North Korea's nuclear weapons program—was firmly established in 1994, and was functioning reasonably well until the Bush-Cheney White House shut it down unilaterally, based on lies of the sort later made famous by Tony Blair's fabrication of Saddam Hussein's supposed weapons of mass destruction. Subsequent steps taken by Russia, China, Japan, and both North and South Korea, nearly saved the peace process, and set the pace for a peaceful reunification of the Koreas. Again, however, Bush, Cheney, and then Obama intervened to crush that effort, in favor of confrontation and military build up for war.

The Agreed Framework

North Korea had been a member of the Non-Proliferation of Nuclear Weapons Treaty (NPT) since 1985, but the International Atomic Energy Agency IAEA) believed in the early 1990s that Pyongyang was hiding some quantity of plutonium (produced at its graphite-moderated nuclear reactor) from IAEA inspectors. A back-and-forth took place with the IAEA and the Clin-

wikipedia

The 5 MWe experimental Magnox reactor of the Yongbyon Nuclear Scientific Research Center, North Korea.

ton Administration, leading to a serious threat from Washington, then represented by Clinton's Defense Secretary William Perry, that a military strike was being planned to take out the Yongbyon nuclear plant which produced the plutonium.

Former President Jimmy Carter then made a personal trip to North Korea and met with Kim Il-sung (the supreme leader of North Korea from the time of its creation after World War II), resulting in an agreement to reach a deal with Washington.

World Economic Forum/swiss-image.ch/Remy Steinegger

Former Vice President Dick Cheney

wikipedia

Former Defense Secretary Donald Rumsfeld

Paul Wolfowitz

White House

Former President Barack Obama

In the resulting "Agreed Framework" of October 1994, North Korea agreed to shut down the 5 megawatt (MW) plutonium-generating nuclear plant and stop construction on two others of 50 MW and 200 MW, and the United States and South Korea would provide a 1,000 MW light-water nuclear reactor that would not produce weapons-grade plutonium. Oil would be provided to the North until the new nuclear reactor came on line. Most important, talks toward normalization of relations would take place immediately, and the United States committed to neither use nor threaten to use nuclear weapons against North Korea while the talks were underway (the Korean War of the 1950s never officially ended—an armistice was signed, but never a peace treaty). Both sides agreed that the Korean Peninsula, North and South, would remain free of nuclear weapons. The IAEA would make routine inspections of the North to confirm compliance.

In 1998, Kim Dae-jung was elected President of South Korea. He had been a leading opponent of the conservative governments in Seoul, was imprisoned several times, and had even been condemned to death at one point. But circumstances changed, and he was elected. He moved immediately to implement a "Sunshine Policy," opening up relations with North Korea. In 2000, he made an historic visit to North Korea and met with supreme leader Kim Jong-il, who had succeeded Kim Il-sung after his father's death in 1994, soon after meeting with Jimmy Carter. Dramatic motion toward peace and cooperation on the Korean peninsula was nearly assured.

Former Defense Secretary Perry has just written, in an April 15 article in *Politico* magazine, that during Clinton's second term, he and others were negotiating a further deal with Pyongyang aimed at a long-term solution for peace on the peninsula. "With allies in South Korea and Japan," Perry wrote, "we discussed a bargain that offered a highly desirable outcome: normalization of relations with North Korea in exchange for its giving up its quest for nuclear weapons. We were tantalizingly close to an agreement, including a presidential visit to Pyongyang, when the clock ran out on Clinton's term."

What happened next was one of the most bloodthirsty and insane acts in history. George Bush's Secretary of Defense Colin Powell, who clearly had more sense than his boss, openly declared on March 6, 2001 that the new Administration intended to "engage with North Korea to pick up where President Clinton left off. Some promising elements were left on the table and we will be examining those elements." But the very next day, President Bush—under the influence of his controller, Vice-President Dick Cheney, and with support from Defense Secretary Donald Rumsfeld and Rumsfeld's deputy —snubbed the visiting South Korean President Kim Dae-jung, announced that there would be no engagement with "dictator" Kim Jung-il (sound familiar?), and essentially scrapped the entire Agreed Framework.

Cheney, Rumsfeld, and Wolfowitz were, of course, the team of neoconservatives that gave us the war on

North-South Korea Rail Connections

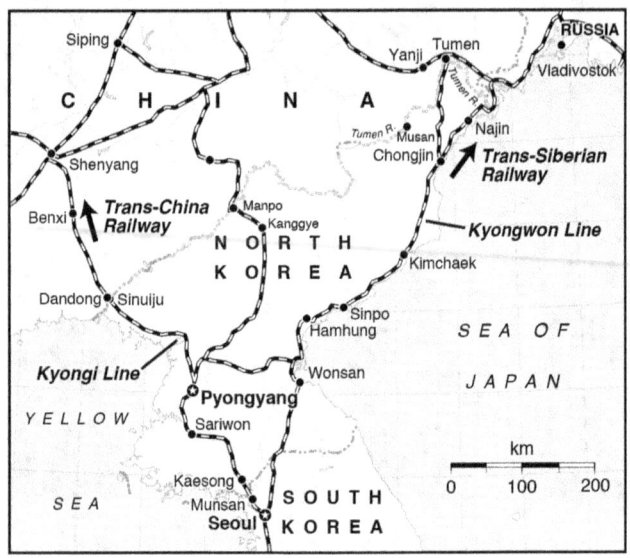

EIRNS/John Sigerson

Iraq on false pretenses, based on Tony Blair's lies, unleashing the destruction of Southwest Asia.

The result of this insanity can be seen today—North Korea now has an estimated 10-20 nuclear weapons. This should not be seen as a terrible blunder by the neocons: It must be seen as their intention. As long as North Korea could be presented as a threat, the United States' expansion of military power in a ring around China could be maintained and expanded. The British imperial division of the world, East against West, could be sustained.

Progress Without British/U.S. Support

President Kim Dae-jung was undaunted in his pursuit of the Sunshine Policy towards North Korea. At the time, Lyndon LaRouche and representatives of his movement were meeting regularly with people in and around Kim Dae-jung's administration, promoting the idea initiated by LaRouche in 1992 called the "New Silk Road." The concept, following the collapse of the Soviet Union, was that a series of economic development corridors connecting Europe and Asia through high-speed rail lines—passing through Russia and the Central Asian republics—would create the conditions for "peace through development," uniting former adversaries in mutually beneficial infrastructure and investment projects. From the beginning of this initiative, LaRouche identified the New Silk Road as proceeding from "Pusan to Rotterdam," noting the importance of resolving the conflict on the Korean peninsula through mutual development between North and South Korea, together with Russia, China and Japan.

In 2002 this effort nearly achieved success, when the two Koreas opened the gates dividing North and South, began clearing the land mines on both sides of the Demilitarized Zone (DMZ), and began rebuilding the severed rail connections between North and South.

The September 27, 2002 issue of *EIR* carried an article by *EIR*'s Kathy Wolfe, who had been organizing for LaRouche's ideas in South Korea, which read:

At 11 a.m. on Sept. 18, North and South Korea cut open the DMZ barbed-wire fences which have divided them for 50 years, in ground-breaking ceremonies to rebuild the "Iron Silk Road"— the trans-Korean rail and road links severed since the Korean War.

In the west, where the Seoul-Pyongyang Kyongui line is being rebuilt toward China, South Korean soldiers unlocked the ten-foot-high fence that runs the 250-kilometer length of the DMZ, at Dorasan Station in Paju, as thousands applauded. Simultaneously, 14.2 kilometers to the north, North Korea opened its fence at Kaesong Station. On the peninsula's east coast, where the Donghae-Wonsan line is being rebuilt toward Russia's Vladivostok, North Korean Prime Minister Hong Song-nam, Railway Minister Kim Yong-sam, and 3,000 guests cut the north fence of the DMZ at Onjong-ri at the foot of Mt. Kumgang (Diamond Mountain). Some 27 km to the south, South Korea opened its east coast fence in Kosung at the Unification Observatory, as crowds gazed north toward the revered Diamond Mountain.

At all four points, ceremonies with fireworks and music exploded. ... They joined a chorus singing the emotional "Our Wish Is Unification," as a train decked with a unification flag and flowers rolled slowly toward the fence where the rails end. ...

In more ceremonies on Sept. 19, construction began: South and North Korean soldiers simultaneously entered the DMZ at all four points for mine-clearing operations. Near Dorasan, 50 soldiers with live ammunition and 50 engineering troops followed a German-made mine-sweeper

At 11 a.m. on September 18, 2002, North and South Korea cut open the Demilitarized Zone (DMZ) barbed-wire fences which had divided them for 50 years, in a ground-breaking ceremony to rebuild the "Iron Silk Road"—the trans-Korean rail and road links that had been severed since the Korean War.

along the rail lines in a massed procession of trucks, backhoes, bulldozers, and an ambulance.

The two Kims, from the North and the South, also set up an industrial complex in the northern city of Kaesong, near the border; South Korean companies set up factories with North Korean employees, benefitting both sides and setting a course for closer cooperation. They also arranged for family visits; members of families long separated by the division of the country after World War II were able to visit each other.

Other stirrings toward peace had taken place just days before these events, when Japanese Prime Minister Junichiro Koizumi travelled to Pyongyang on September 17, 2002, to meet with Kim Jong-il. The two issued full apologies to each other—Japan for its invasion and occupation of Korea from 1910 to 1945, and North Korea for the abduction of eleven Japanese citizens. They also agreed to formal diplomatic normalization talks, to begin in October.

Russian President Vladimir Putin, who had held several summits with both Kim Jong-il and Koizumi leading up to the meeting, offered his full support for the New Silk Road process.

At the same time, China initiated six-party talks among the two Koreas, Russia, China, Japan, and the United States. It was hoped that the rail connections linking South Korea to China and Russia through North Korea would be up and runnng by the end of 2003, and that the road to reunification would lie just ahead. It was not to be.

Subverting the Six-Party Talks

The Bush Administration launched its war against Afghanistan in 2002 and another against Iraq in 2003. Over the next fourteen years, Bush and Obama would keep the United States in a state of permanent warfare, targetting the three secular nations in Southwest Asia—Iraq, Libya, and Syria—none of which was Islamist, while all were firmly anti-terror. These two Anglophile presidents also sustained the longest war in United States history, continuing still today, in Afghanistan.

In his 2002 State of the Union Address, as Japanese and South Korean leaders were meeting with North Korean leaders and preparing joint development projects, George W. Bush pronounced that North Korea was part of an "Axis of Evil," together with Iraq and Iran.

As former Secretary of Defense Perry said in the article quoted above, the North Korean leadership may be reckless, but it is "not crazy or suicidal." It would never use its nuclear weapons offensively, he noted, since it knows "the American response would bring death to the leadership and devastation to its country." To that must be added that Pyongyang is fully aware of what happened to both Iraq and Libya, which gave up their nuclear weapons programs voluntarily, only to then be bombed mercilessly, their leaders killed, and their countries left in the hands of warring terrorist factions. North Korea will never give up its nuclear weapons program unless it has normalized relations with the United States and has obtained a non-aggression pledge. This is in fact what Perry recommends to President Trump.

As in Southwest Asia, so also in East Asia: Bush and Obama played along with the six-party talks, but found

chosonexchange.org

Rason-Russia railway link extends a standard gauge train line all the way to Rajin port (just south of Najin on map).

every excuse to claim—almost always falsely—that North Korea was cheating. On this false basis, Obama imposed more and more sanctions while deploying more and more military forces into the region. Obama then officially adopted a policy called "strategic patience," which really meant refusing all contact, increasing sanctions every time Pyongyang tested a missile or nuclear weapon, and "patiently" waiting for either a collapse of the regime or an excuse to start a war. As with Bush's policy, it was an assured failure, by intention, aimed at justifying the build-up around China.

Obama's "Pivot to Asia" was the most blatant case of this fraud. The claim that the Pivot, and his later deployment of THAAD missile systems to South Korea, were meant to deter North Korea, fooled neither Beijing nor Moscow. Under the Pivot policy, Obama deployed massive U.S. military power in a ring around China and the Russian Far East, while the Trans-Pacific Partnership (TPP) trade policy was openly aimed at isolating China and slowing down its increasing dominance of economic relations in the region. This attempt at economic isolation was a colossal failure, since China was at the same time implementing Xi Jinping's New Silk Road policy (the Belt and Road Initiative), bringing real development, not military coercion, to the nations of the region.

Sad Case of Park Geun-Hye

The other major tragedy brought on by Obama's role in Asia was the destruction of President Park Geun-hye's government in South Korea. Park is the daughter of Park Chung-hee, the leader who transformed South Korea during his presidency, from 1961-1979, from one of the poorest nations on Earth after the Korean war to what is today one of the leading industrial powers. His daughter Geun-hye was not a strong leader, but she had a vision, which she called "the Eurasian Vision," that Korea, together with Russia and China, would play a key role in the development of the entire Eurasian continent. In September 2015, she attended the celebration of victory in World War II in Beijing, standing proudly on the podium with Xi Jinping and Vladimir Putin.

Clearly this Eurasian Vision required a peaceful resolution of the conflict with North Korea, so that the rail and other connections between South Korea and Russia and China could be restored. It was also understood that South Korean technology and skilled North Korean labor could, together, contribute to the much needed development of the Russian Far East, to the benefit of all.

In fact, although her government maintained a "no official contact" policy towards the North, she had allowed an extraordinary consortium to be established between Russia, North Korea, and three leading companies in the South—Hyundai Merchant Marine, a logistics and container freight company; Posco, the largest South Korean steel company; and Korail, the Korean state rail corporation. The consortium sent Russian coal by rail to a new port structure built in the North Korean city of Rason, where it was shipped by Hyundai Merchant Marine to South Korea, then by Korail trains to Posco steel mills. This was in fact the model for a system of state-industry cooperation which could have led to a "peace through development" solution.

Then, in January 2016, after the fourth North Korean nuclear weapons test (a test that everyone knew would happen eventually for the reasons given above), President Park Geun-hye capitulated totally to the Obama

THAAD missile defense system launch.

Missile Defense Agency

policy. Not only did she order the closure of the consortium of North Korea, Russia, and the South Korean corporations, but she even closed the Kaesong Industrial Complex, which by this time was employing more than 50,000 North Koreans in 123 South Korean companies.

This left virtually no ties between North and South—political, economic, or social. While the legal removal of President Park from power through impeachment was not specifically over this policy, but over corruption issues internal to South Korea, the impeachment was nonetheless aided by her obvious failure, and weakness, in letting Obama's policies poison Seoul's relations with China, Russia, and North Korea, creating the threat of a war provoked by the United States—a war that would be devastating to South Korea.

The election to replace Park will be held May 9, creating the potential for a new approach.

Trump Rejects the Imperial Divide

The Trump campaign made very clear that he intended to be friends with Russia, much to the horror of London and the warmongers in both the Democratic and Republican parties. Although he was critical of China's economic policies during the campaign, he has now established a close relationship with Xi Jinping,

including their personal meeting in Florida in April.

Trump's bombing of a Syrian airbase on April 6 went against his pledge to end Bush's and Obama's wars of aggression against nations which were no threat to our own and was a clear violation of international law. But it was done on the basis of lies provided by British intelligence, claiming to have proof that the Assad government was responsible for a chemical weapon attack—a total absurdity.

Similarly, British Foreign Secretary Boris Johnson has been screaming for war against Syria and goading Trump to prepare for a preemptive attack on North Korea. Even if North Korea's nuclear weapons were destroyed in a first strike, its conventional weapons could, and likely would, totally destroy the beautiful city of Seoul, only 35 miles from the well-fortified border, and other sites in South Korea.

Although it would be an act of lunacy to launch such an attack on North Korea, and it is highly unlikely that Trump could be induced to do so, there will be no solution to the conflict until the British are acknowledged as the source of the crisis, aiming to prevent President Trump from carrying out his expressed intention to bring the United States into a new relationship with both China and Russia.

The Russian Deputy Permanent Representative to the UN, Vladimir Safronkov, responded on April 12 to a typically virulent rant against both Syria and Russia by the British Permanent Representative Matthew Rycroft, CBE (Commander of the Order of the British Empire), in a manner which profoundly located the fundamental intention of the British Empire:

"The essence is," Safronkov said, "and everyone in the UN knows this very well, is that you are afraid, you have been losing sleep, over the fact that we might be working together with the United States, cooperating with the United States—that is your fear. You are doing everything to make sure that this kind of cooperation be undermined."

Safronkov's statement is accurate. He is perhaps the first world leader to identify what Lyndon LaRouche has identified for more than 50 years: The British will stop at nothing to prevent the United States from breaking the imperial divide between West and East and creating with Russia and China the basis for a new paradigm based on the common aims of mankind.

Now is the time to make that break, to establish a new era of mankind based on development, and end the British Empire once and for all.

Every Day Counts In Today's Showdown To Save Civilization

That's why you need EIR's **Daily Alert Service**, a strategic overview compiled with the input of Lyndon LaRouche, and delivered to your email 5 days a week.

The election of Donald Trump to the Presidency of the Untied States has launched a new global era whose character has yet to be determined. The Obama-Clinton drive toward confrontation with Russia has been disrupted--but what will come next?

Over the next weeks and months there will be a pitched battle to determine the course of the Trump Administration. Will it pursue policies of cooperation with Russia and China in the New Silk Road, as the President-Elect has given some signs of? Will it follow through against Wall Street with Glass-Steagall?

The opposition to these policies will be fierce. If there is to be a positive outcome to this battle, an informed citizenry must do its part--intervening, educating, inspiring. That's why you need the EIR Daily Alert more than ever.

TUESDAY, NOVEMBER 22, 2016

Volume 3, Number 65

EIR Daily Alert Service

P.O. BOX 17390, WASHINGTON, DC 20041-0390

- Only Global Solutions, Based on New Principles, Can Work
- Tulsi Gabbard Meets with Donald Trump Regarding Syria
- Robert Kagan Throws in the Towel, Complains U.S. Is Becoming 'Solipsistic'
- War Party Moving To Preempt Trump-Putin Reset
- Syrian Army Makes More Progress in Aleppo
- Duterte Gives OK to Nuclear Power for Philippines
- Europe Will Suffer from Maintaining Russia Sanctions
- Former Chilean Diplomat Confirmed, 'We Will Joyfully Welcome Xi Jinping'
- Duterte and Putin Establish Philippines-Russia Cooperation
- François Fillon, Pro-Russian Thatcherite, Wins First Round of French Right-Wing Presidential Primary

EDITORIAL

Only Global Solutions, Based on New Principles, Can Work

II. A Dialogue of Civilizations

The Belt And Road Initiative, The World Land-Bridge, and Corresponding Ideas in Western and Chinese Culture

On April 13 and 14, the Schiller Institute, in cooperation with the China Energy Fund Committee and the Foundation for the Revival of Classical Culture, held an international conference in Manhattan, on the theme of the Belt and Road Initiative, the World Land-Bridge, and corresponding ideas in Western and Chinese culture. This conference and an associated evening concert brought together well over 200 participants, including high-level representatives of crucial nations, including:

• Dr. Patrick Ho of the China Energy Fund Committee,

• Mme. Meifang Zhang, the Deputy Consul General of the People's Republic of China, in New York,

• Mr. Petr Ilyichev, the Chargé d'Affaires of the Permanent Mission to the United Nations of the Russian Federation, and

• Mr. Faiyaz Kazi, Counselor to the Permanent Mission to the United Nations of Bangladesh.

The conference was opened by Helga Zepp-La-Rouche, founder of the Schiller Institutes, accompanied by presentations by top representatives of China and Russia. These presentations marked the stark contrast in outlook between the potential for the tremendous economic growth and cooperation of the World Land-Bridge concept, as led up to now by China, and the contrasting drive for war coming from the British Empire.

The Chinese and Russian representatives were greeted very warmly by the assembled audience, showing the potential for the better America to ally with these great nations. This opening panel was covered in the previous, April 21 issue of *EIR*.

A panel of presentations on the development aspects of the Belt and Road Initiative followed. These included:

• A discussion of Lyndon LaRouche's economic concepts as applied to infrastructure as a platform,

• The programs for integrating the Americas into the Belt and Road Initiative,

• The stunning success China has had in becoming the world's leader in high-speed rail,

• The potential for southern Asian integration with the example of Bangladesh, the most densely populated nation on the globe,

• The energy requirements for full development,

• The long-term maintenance and physical sustainability needs for a project of such immense scale and duration, and

The need for an outlook toward space infrastructure as a driver for mankind as a whole.

These presentations fleshed out and further developed the concepts presented in the opening of the conference. The potential is real, and the benefits are absolutely tremendous, if we throw off the British yoke and cooperate for mutual benefit. This second conference panel will be reported in the coming, May 5 issue of *EIR*.

The third panel took on the deeper issue of the dialogue of cultures on the highest level. What are the greatest ideas of western and Chinese civilizations, which can serve as a basis for the most elevated dialogue? Reports on the third panel follow here, along with other, complementary articles on the same broad theme.

A half-hour summary video of the conference can be found at: https://youtu.be/Eq9NmsQG9xQ

EIR's YouTube channel is here: https://www.youtube.com/channel/UCQJe_Wd7vFqKJXfJWov9xmg

Subscribe to *EIR*'s channel here: https://www.youtube.com/channel/UCQJe_Wd7vFqKJXfJWov9xmg?sub_confirmation=1

BERTRAND RUSSELL'S WORST NIGHTMARE

Dialogue of Cultures: The Content of Strategy Is the Method Used to Make It

by Dennis Speed

April 25—Even as British Defense secretary Sir Michael Fallon made the lunatic statement on BBC radio's April 24 "Today" program that, "In the most extreme circumstances, we have made it very clear that you can't rule out the use of nuclear weapons as a first strike," saner forces had already moved to replace his geopolitical arguments for self-extinction with a human idea of durable survival for the planet as a whole.

The Schiller Institute, in cooperation with the China Energy Fund Committee and the Foundation for the Revival of Classical Culture, had provided a forum for discussion by scholars, scientists, engineers, diplomats, and citizens, of the possibility for a new cultural platform, a higher conceptual level congruent with the "Belt and Road Initiative" of China—a kind of cultural New Silk Road. Several conference panelists argued that this was the "cognitive height" from which the mutual interest of all of humanity should be simultaneously addressed, rather than allow "brutish" empires to conduct preventive war, an international war crime as defined at Nuremberg, but apparently not acknowledged by the British Defense Secretary.

The first panel of the two-day, April 13-14 Manhattan conference on "U.S.-China Cooperation on the Belt and Road Initiative and Corresponding Ideas in Chinese and Western Philosophy," was published in our previous issue, dated April 21. The scientifically important second panel of the first day, "Engineering the New

EIRNS/Jason Ross
Dennis Speed

Silk Road," will be covered in our forthcoming May 5 issue. The section in this *EIR* covers the second day's proceedings, along with other articles on the same theme.

On April 14, covered in this issue, the founder of the Schiller Institutes, Helga Zepp-LaRouche, known for two decades as "the Silk Road Lady" for her tireless campaign for what has now become known worldwide as the "New Silk Road/One Belt One Road" policy, spoke on the topic: "The Ideal of Highest Humanity: the Common Philosophical Foundations of Western and Asian Culture." At the opening of her presentation, Zepp-LaRouche revealed the epistemological root of the irreconcilable nature of the conflict between the forces of civilization, and the British Empire:

The Schiller Institute had from the very beginning the idea that you had to have a just, new world economic order. . . . The hope-filled vision of President Xi Jinping for what he always calls "a community of the shared future of mankind," which he conceptualized along with the "Win-Win" cooperation of the New Silk Road, has recently been adopted in a resolution of the UN Security Council, which means that it is now officially—even if in any case it had been that already—it's now an overarching principle, which binds all nations of this world to this higher perspective. With this concept, for the first time, a strategic initiative has been put on the agenda which can replace war-causing geopolitics, with the ideal of an united humanity.

In the three and one half years since Xi Jinping proposed this, in Kazakhstan in September 2013, this policy, this idea, has rapidly become widespread, and inspired more and more nations, particularly among the less developed nations. It has promoted an optimism that was previously absent, optimism that in the near future poverty can be overcome and that humane conditions of life for all people on this planet can be created. Countless people from different nations and cultures perceive that we are standing at the beginning of a new epoch of universal history.

But why is it that so many governments and heads of state and politicians and broadminded people recognize in an instant the enormous potential embodied in it to define the common goals of humanity from the standpoint of the future—while others state that there must be "hidden reasons" behind the Belt and Road Initiative, that there are sinister motives from China, replacing one imperialism with another one, this time a Chinese one? How is it possible, that the same factual object—namely, that the concrete development concept for all of humanity is being realized, comes only to be interpreted in such completely different ways? These opposing points of view obviously have to do with the different axioms of thinking from which this question is approached.

Zepp-LaRouche's and Mike Billington's presentations on Day Two of the conference, forcefully introduced the German thinkers Gottfried Leibniz, the true inventor of the science of physical economy, and Cardinal Nicholas of Cusa, the man who, through his scientific method of "negative theology," as demonstrated in his work *On Learned Ignorance*, revolutionized all of Western thought. Cusa and Leibniz were, in contradistinction to Bertrand Russell (whose 1922 book, *The Problem of China*, had afflicted both Chinese and non-Chinese with mutual cultural misperceptions for decades), the carriers of the Platonic tradition that asserts that there are no limits to human creativity—and there-

EIRNS/Jason Ross

Dr. Patrick Ho (left) and Helga Zepp-LaRouche.

fore no limits to growth.

A lively discussion was undertaken in the question and answer session with the China Energy Fund Committee's Patrick Ho, who, in his wide-ranging speech—which discussed the *I Ching* (Yijing), Confucian thought, and Lao Tze (Laozi)—asserted that Chinese thinkers had often "done what Europe did before Europe" in several areas of science.

Zepp-LaRouche and Billington clearly differed from Dr. Ho's conception of what he termed "Western thought." Billington, in particular, insisted that both British and British-influenced Chinese figures had either intentionally suppressed or completely misunderstood the true contributions of thinkers such as Leibniz, both in Europe and in Asia, and it was the war between epistemologies and worldviews that must be understood, rather than an apocryphal geographic "cultural divide."

A conference attendee asking a question during a dialogue period, following the presentations of one of the sessions.

Free Humanity from Rule by Empire

The implications of this particular discussion for international strategy are enormous, perhaps even existential. For centuries, British East India Company employees, such as John Locke, David Hume, Adam Smith, and Thomas Malthus have been identified as "thinkers," and British empiricism, both in the form of induction and deduction, has been the "coin of the realm" (the British realm) in American education.

What Americans call "practical thinking" often involves depending on the methods devised by these lackeys of the Crown to determine "what is real and what is not." This was not the method of thinking used by Benjamin Franklin, Alexander Hamilton, Edgar Allan Poe, or Lyndon LaRouche. They rejected the British method of argument. Franklin was a follower of Leibniz. (And, as researcher David Wang pointed out in a surprising and original presentation Friday on "The Confucian Influence on Ben Franklin and the American Revolution," Franklin was well aware of Chinese philosophy and thought.) The United States, as a consequence, led the world in discoveries and inventions, and built the world's greatest economy as a result.

It is that capacity which the British know will suddenly return to the United States if it joins Russia and China in the Belt and Road Initiative. Therefore, British ideology, what Winston Churchill once called "the Empire of the Mind," is the battleground today for the soul of the United States, and of its Presidency.

Those in the United States who remain either baffled, dismissive, or merely cynical as to why the Trump Administration—which had clearly stated its opposition to "Project Democracy"-style regime change policies applied to Syria one week earlier—would then bomb Syria on April 6 (the same day that President Trump's meeting with Chinese Premier Xi Jinping took place), might do well, or at least better, to consider the axioms now in play in the American mind. These are axioms that did not exist in the American mind, in this form, one hundred years ago. These are the axioms, leading to actions, that allowed that event, which in fact reversed without explanation the just-pronounced policy of the White House, to supplant that announced policy as though it had never been uttered. In order to assist the reader in unearthing that normally invisible lattice-work of axioms that render current history incomprehensible for nearly all Americans, consider the following to be "facts":

• The primary actual allies of the United States in the world today are Russia and China.

• The primary actual enemy of the United States and of humanity, is the British Empire, and its post-industrial geopolitical strategy for population reduction.

• The "New Silk Road," "One Belt One Road," and "Belt and Road Initiative" policy evolutions that have been proposed by the Chinese government, each with greater clarity and precision, are fully convergent with the "American System" policies of Abraham Lincoln, Franklin Roosevelt, and John F. Kennedy, particularly Kennedy's "Apollo Project" space-exploration orientation. Each of those American policies has been a realization, with greater or lesser degrees of success, of the policies enunciated in Alexander Hamilton's Four Reports, on manufactures, credit, and the National Bank. By nature, all "Hamiltonian" policies oppose the continued existence of the British Empire, as did, in fact,

Lincoln, FDR, and JFK.

• "Green policies," such as those laughably identified as the "true science" of global warming, are frauds deployed against the science of high energy-density technologies (such as advanced-design nuclear power reactors and thermonuclear fusion). The purpose of advocacy of replacing fossil fuels with backward solar and wind, which are low-energy density forms of technology, is to argue for the "regrettable necessity" for forced population reduction to "save the planet," by

Why You Can't See the British Empire at Work? Because You Are Looking Right at It!

On Jan. 21, just one day after President Trump was inaugurated, the UK's *Spectator* magazine ran an online article by Paul Wood entitled, "Will Donald Trump be Assassinated, Ousted in a Coup, or Just Impeached?"

As you will see below, this is British Policy, directly from the Monarchy itself, stated by Her Majesty's own ministers or her Imperial media mouthpieces, and what is reported here is just the last two weeks.

The UK's *Evening Standard* reported on April 11 that UK Foreign Minister Boris Johnson, attending the G7 meeting in Italy, pushed for a regime change policy in Syria. The *Standard* reported, "The summit united on a call for Assad to step down, and to send a message to Russian President Vladimir Putin that he must choose between aligning with the west or being tied to the dictator."

The *Standard* then states, based on anonymous sources who apparently speak on behalf of the United States, " 'The American view is that Assad can go the nice way, which is that the Russians drop him, or the bad way, which is the Libyan example,' said a source referring to the death of Libyan despot Muammar Gaddafi at the hands of a mob in 2011."

Yet, this contradicts U.S. Secretary of State Rex Tillerson's public comments on national television just days earlier, when he said, "We've seen what that looks like, when you undertake a violent regime change in Libya, and the situation in Libya continues to be very chaotic. We have to learn the lessons of the past and learn the lessons of what went wrong in Libya when you choose that pathway of regime change."

Regime change is not the American view, certainly not the American people, and also not the President's policy, rather, it is what the UK wishes the American view to be, so that its war crimes will be carried out by others, much like they deployed Hitler for war with Russia.

On April 17, the UK's *Independent* reported that the UK's Attorney General, Queen's Counsel Jeremy Wright, claimed that the legal case against Tony Blair, based on the British Parliament's Chilcot report—a report which investigated and proved Blair's role in the illegal Iraq war—is a hopeless case "because the crime of aggression does not exist in English law, even though it does exist in international law."

The UN Charter, in this case based on the Nuremberg or London Charter which made the case against aggressive warfare following WWII, states in Article 2, paragraph 4, "All Members shall refrain in their international relations from the threat or use of force against the territorial integrity or political independence of any state, or in any other manner inconsistent with the Purposes of the United Nations."

The UK is declaring itself above international law, or rather, asserting its tradition of Imperial Law, a law above nations. Tony Blair was his Queen's Prime Minister, and the Monarchy's power for assassination as with Gaddafi, illegal war as in Iraq and Libya, or coup d'état as in Ukraine in 2014, is the Monarchy's publicly stated criminal foreign policy.

Then on April 24, the UK's *Independent* again weighed in regarding the question of aggressive war, this time by Her Majesty's Defense Minister Michael Fallon. He stated, in response to the discussion on the UK's Trident Nuclear Missile program that, "In the most extreme circumstances, we have made it very clear that you can't rule out the use of nuclear weapons as a first strike."

Regime change, aggressive warfare, and the first use of nuclear weapons are British policy.

reducing world population to less than 1-2 billion people. It is believed by the present generation of British anti-civilizationalists that only under such a condition could the present, "Darwinian" geopolitical world order dominated by the British Empire in the form of the British Commonwealth of nations, the "Five Eyes" intelligence arrangement, and the defunct NATO military alliance, stand a chance of "maintaining world order."

In the days that followed the April 13-15 conference, as participants returned from the two-day gathering, the deeper impact of the uniqueness and urgency of the approach that Helga Zepp-LaRouche, Lyndon LaRouche, and others have fought for in the form of the World-Land-Bridge—against the geopolitics of the dying, failed British Empire—becomes increasingly evident.

Consider, for example, the somber implication for the future of geopolitics of the following announcement published by the Xinhua news agency and covered by *EIR*:

To "promote innovation and cooperation in space exploration," Xinhua reports, China yesterday created a "coalition," initiated by the Chinese Society of Astronautics and the Northwestern Polytechnical University in Xi'an, which involves forty-eight universities, research institutes, and academic organizations, both domestic and from abroad. Its purpose, explained Tian Yulong, Secretary-General of the China National Space Administration, is to "boost exchanges in space innovation between its members, and help joint training of high-caliber professionals." China is already giving access to its space technology, such as its Beidou navigation satellite system, to countries along the Silk Road. Joint satellite projects have been under discussion."

What does such a "Silk Road in Space" do to the "geopolitical," "geostrategic" computer "war simulations" of the thermonuclear maniacs, the British liberal imperialists, and their ilk? What happens when the "Eurasian heartland" is also located above the heartland—in space? What happens when the "ocean power" of your empire has to take into consideration successfully sailing the five layers of the earth's atmosphere, not to mention joint collaboration with nations on and around the Moon?

Astronaut Jack Fischer, speaking along with fellow astronaut Peggy Whitson to President Donald Trump on April 24 from the International Space Station, excitedly said this:

I launched a Russian vehicle with my Russian friend [Cosmonaut Fyodor Yurchikhin] from Kazakhstan, got the immediate perspective changed, as we got to orbit and I saw that frail thin blue line of life around the Earth; six hours later we're docked to the station; the next day I install an experiment in the Japanese module that's going to be looking at new drugs, and how we can make those drugs for muscular dystrophy, Alzheimer's, drug-resistant bacteria, all those sorts of things; a couple of hours later I watched our crewmate Thomas Pesquet, a Frenchman, drive a Canadian robotic arm to capture a spaceship from Virginia, carrying three-and-a-half tons of cargo and science that's going to keep us busy for the next few months and dock that to the station.

Sir, it's amazing. Oh, and then, now I'm talking to the President of the United States, while hanging from a wall—it's amazing. The International Space Station is by far the best example of international cooperation and what we can do when we work together, in the history of humanity. And I am so proud to be a part of it.

The Silk Road in space, an incipient realization of the fourth of LaRouche's Four Laws policy, if advocated vigorously as we approach the May 14-15 Beijing summit, and the subsequent May 29 one-hundredth birthday of President John Kennedy, would be the perfect answer to the "mad dogs and British imperialists" that would lose the whole world, and their souls, for the greater glory of a false idea of empire, an idea whose time has gone.

The United States, still the pre-eminent nation in space, could re-enter the domain of greatness by invoking JFK's Apollo project, this time including the crash development of thermonuclear fusion power, necessary for travel to Mars, and for electrical power on Earth as well. If the United States should extend itself to all nations, and thus lift itself out of the hell of British imperial slavery to once again occupy its once-proud position as a beacon of hope for all humanity, the angry but impotent British Empire will stomp its feet, rip itself in two, and, like Rumpelstiltskin, disappear forever.

East and West: A Dialogue of Great Cultures

by Helga Zepp-LaRouche

Mrs. LaRouche's address to Panel II, the Dialogue of Civilizations, of the Schiller Institute conference entitled "The Belt and Road Initiative—and Corresponding Ideas in Chinese and Western Philosophy," in New York City on April 14, 2017. Her remarks are preceded by a brief introduction by the moderator, Dennis Speed.

Dennis Speed: This conference originates in a conversation that happened between two of the presenters on the occasion of an earlier conference that we held. There was a proposal that there should be a conference which would take up the Belt and Road Initiative, but should also begin a process of a more in-depth dialogue: Not merely on the question of East versus West, but on the common thread of humanity, which is really what characterizes the New Silk Road proposal we're making, and the old Silk Road, which was the pride of China, exemplifies. Over the course of the past three decades, Helga LaRouche has made the point over and over, that the primary problem of humanity is that it is not grown up. That doesn't mean that at certain points there have not been adults in humanity, and there have not been people who exemplified creativity, but we wanted to take the occasion today, to give you some idea about these areas.

So, to begin, I'm introducing to you the founder and chairwoman of the Schiller Institute, Helga Zepp-LaRouche.

Helga Zepp-LaRouche: Dear friends of Classical music and Classical culture and the Schiller Institute: The Schiller Institute from the very beginning had the idea that you have to have a Just New World Economic Order, but that it would not ever work if it were not connected with a renaissance of Classical culture. What I'm going to talk about, the topic I'm speaking about, is the idea of highest humanity, the common philosophical foundations of Western and Asian culture—you will see what I mean.

The hope-filled vision of President Xi Jin-ping for what he always calls a community of shared future of mankind, which he conceptualized along with the "win-win" cooperation of the New Silk Road, has recently been adopted in a resolution of the UN Security Council. Which means that it is now officially—even if in any case it has been that already—it's now an over-arching principle which binds all nations of this world through this higher perspective. With this concept, for the first time, a strategic initiative has been put on the agenda which can replace the war-causing geopolitics with the ideal of a united humanity. In the three-and-a-half years since Xi Jinping proposed this policy in Kazakhstan, in September [2013], this idea has rapidly become widespread and inspired more and more nations. Particularly among the less-developed nations, it has promoted a previously completely absent optimism that in the near future poverty can be overcome, and that humane conditions of life for all people on this planet can be created. Countless people from different nations and cultures perceive that we are standing at the beginning of a new epoch of universal history.

UN photo/Loey Felipe

President of the People's Republic of China Xi Jinping, addressing the UN General Assembly Sept. 28, 2015.

But why is it that so many governments and heads of state and politicians and broad-minded people recognize in an instant the enormous potential embodied in it to define the common goals of humanity from the standpoint of the future, while others state, that there must be hidden reasons behind the Belt and Road Initiative, that there are sinister motives by China, replacing one imperialism with another one; this time a Chinese one. How is it possible that the same factual object, namely, that a concrete development concept for all of humanity is being realized, only to be interpreted in such completely different ways? These opposing points of view obviously have to do with the different axioms of thinking from which this question is approached.

The former publisher of the London *Times* and one of the leading mouthpieces of the British Empire, Lord [William] Rees-Mogg, once criticized the theses of Samuel Huntington that it will be unavoidable to come to a clash of civilizations between Christianity, Islam, Hinduism, and Confucianism. He advanced the notion that the real conflict would play out between the old values of Christianity, Islam, Hinduism, and Confucianism and the new values of the New Age neo-liberal society and modernity.

Post-Christian Values

Russian Foreign Minister Sergey Lavrov, in his recent annual press conference, made a similar point regarding the values of the free West, which it relentlessly tries to impose on all non-Western countries. "These are probably not the values espoused by the grandfathers of today's Europeans," said Lavrov, "but something new and modernized, a free-for-all, I would say. They are radically and fundamentally at odds with the values handed down from generation to generation for centuries in our country—which we would like to cherish and hand down to our children and grandchildren.

When during foreign policy battles, we and many others face a demand to accept these new post-Christian Western values, including permissiveness and universality of liberal approaches to the life of the individual, I think it is indecent on a human level, but in terms of professional diplomats, it's a colossal mistake and a completely unacceptable overestimation of your influence on international relations."

It is self-evident that geopolitics and the notion of a unipolar world, also the imposition of Western values, must be replaced with a real dialogue of cultures. But how should a real understanding take place between philosophies and art forms from completely different cultures, which are separated from one another by different languages, traditions, and customs? Does one need a new lingua franca, or pop songs in English, Hindi, Arabic, or Chinese in order to understand each other? Or is there something more profound, universal, belonging to all cultures? And without abusing in the least their uniqueness, which puts them in the position for a real exchange, and allows reciprocal enrichment, a kind of cultural "win-win" harmony?

Much confusion regarding this issue has come into being because the characterization of foreign cultures is often not presented in a positive light, or at least objectively. Historians and culture experts of colonial powers always insisted on maintaining the right of interpretation; not only of their own, but also of foreign cultural histories.

As a result, many Europeans and Americans know very little about the best of Asian cultures, while the Asians often only get to know the British interpretation of European history. In European intellectual history for the past 2.5 thousand years, two fundamentally opposed directions have been in conflict, which one could describe as the battle between the oligarchical system and the republican system for the common good. The view of man of the first, associated with Sparta and Lycurgus, claims that all privileges are for the ruling elite; and it denies to the broad masses the right to mental and material development. Thus they remain subjects easier to rule over. The second considers all people as capable of potentially endless perfection, and sees it as the duty of the state to promote, in the best possible way, the creative capability of its citizens.

The most important of the various Western versions of the first, the oligarchical model, based themselves on a more or less mechanistic comprehension of the world in the tradition of Aristotle, which does not allow real qualitative advancement. The second, the progressive model, oriented to the common good, is based on the wise Solon of Athens, who saw the purpose of humanity in its progressive motion, but especially in Plato: thinkers in his tradition grasped that humans, thanks to their creative reason, are continually capable of formulating adequate hypotheses on the lawfulness of the universe, which potentially leads to the limitless deepening of knowledge as well as the development of humanity. Naturally, with the first system, various variations and neuroses emerged; like the Manichean ideology with the idea that good and evil will always exist equally, or the pre-Christian notion of Gaia, with a cyclical notion of development. These forms have survived into the present, in the modern Gaia cult and the Greens.

Two Opposed Western Traditions

But in the end, all forms of appearance of the first system, this policy of empiricism, positivism, scholasticism, the deductive and inductive method, the French and English Enlightenment—for example, Locke, Hobbes, or Newton, up through the critical method of the Frankfurt School or the deconstructionism of the present—are all variations of the Aristotelian tradition. Common to all is the idea that the essential source of knowledge is experience through the senses. Man is evil by nature, and must be controlled by repressive forms of government. And finally, that the world is a closed, limited system.

In contrast, there is the tradition drawing on Plato, including not only such diverse thinkers as St. Augustine, St. Bonaventure, Nicholas of Cusa, Johannes Kepler, Gottfried Leibniz, Gottfried Ephraim Lessing, Friedrich Schiller, and the Humboldt brothers, but also Albert Einstein, Vladimir Vernadsky, and Krafft Ehricke, to just name a few prominent thinkers. These thinkers have in common a fundamental optimism about the role of man in the universe—that human mental creativity is itself a power in the further development of the physical universe and that there is a connection between the harmonic development of all human mental and spiritual capabilities, and the positive development of the commonwealth of the state, and the laws of the Cosmos. Virtually all progress of knowledge in the natural sciences, or great Classical art and European civilization, is uniquely thanks to the Platonic tradition. It is due to the capability of humans *not to be dependent* on random external influences, but to exercise the power of reason, to determine with scientific precision where the next higher qualitative breakthrough to expand knowledge must take place.

wkipedia

Solon of Athens

It is easy to demonstrate that the viewpoint of the critics who impugn China's policy of the New Silk Road with secret motives, is just a projection of their own geopolitical motives onto China. They think like the famous chamber valet described by Hegel in his *Phenomenology of the Mind*, who could only imagine the world-historical individual in his underwear, as he must daily help him dressing and undressing. They are imprisoned by the "new values" spoken of by Rees-Mogg or the post-Christian values for Russia, rejected by Lavrov. They simply cannot imagine that there are people, and even governments, who are truly committed not only to the welfare of their own population, but are also for the harmonic development of all of humanity. They hate the moral claim rising out of this mentality, because it puts into question their alleged right to the principle "everything is allowed."

On the other hand, mutual understanding is easier to achieve when one turns to the philosophers and poets of the optimistic tradition. There, a striking similarity among thinkers is found, though they come out of completely diverse cultural circles, they nonetheless come to the same insights about the nature of man and the purpose of existence. The most auspicious example of this concordance, is that of the philosophical and aesthetical principles of Confucius, whose influence has impacted many parts of Asia, well beyond China, for the past 2,500 years, with those of the great German poet of freedom, Friedrich Schiller, where both dedicated their life's work to the ennoblement of mankind. An important similarity is also found in many aspects of other thinkers such as Mencius, Nicholas of Cusa, Gottfried Leibniz, and Wilhelm von Humboldt. Common to all of these great minds was the tireless struggle with the question of how life together among human beings can be shaped, such that the inherent creative capability within them can unfold in the best way, and be brought into concordance with the world order such that natural law's right to happiness can be attained by all of society.

For Confucius, man is good by nature. Everything bad comes from a lack of development, man has the freedom and the moral obligation to improve himself through an act of his own will. Everything depends on this inner power, as an external evil is by no means always an evil, but to the contrary, a test of character through which he can emerge strengthened and with purer principles. Schiller developed the same thoughts with his concept

A statue of Friedrich Schiller in Belle Isle, Detroit, Michigan.

pinehurst19475

of the sublime—a state of mind which one can attain when one's identity is bound to universal ideas which go beyond our limited physical existence; which yield not a physical, but better, a moral certainty. Also, Schiller emphasized freedom of the will. "All other things *must*; man is the being who *wills,*" said Schiller in his writings on the sublime. "The morally educated man, and only this one, is entirely free. Only the person who has a beautiful character, who finds joy in exercising justice, well-being, moderation, steadfastness, and devotion; and who doesn't lose these qualities even if hit by an array of great misfortunes, is sublime."

Aesthetical Education

For Confucius, the education of personal character is achieved, in addition to literary studies, through the six free arts: learning the rituals, music, archery, charioteering, riding, and mathematics. For him, poetry and music play the most important role, as they broaden the imagination and power of conception. Schiller writes about this in his critique of Berger's poems. He says, "In a time when our mental powers have been compartmentalized, and their effectiveness scattered as a necessary consequence of the expanded scope of our knowledge and the specialization of professions—poetry is virtually unique in its power to re-unify the soul's sundered forces, to occupy the heart and mind, activity and wit, reason and power of imagination, in harmonious alliance, and as it were, to restore the entire human being within us."

According to the *Lunyu*, or *Analects*, from the translation of Richard Wilhelm into German, Confucius fo-

cused his students in the following way: "My young friends! Why are you not engaging yourselves with poetry? *Shijing* [*Classic of Poetry*]: Poetry is congenial to stimulate the imagination. She lets us view life in a contemplative mirror, thus cleansing our emotions. She awakens social nobleness; she arouses anger against injustice and deceitfulness. She permits the emergence in families and in the state of intentions for moral actions, and otherwise broadens our knowledge of the whole organic world; namely, the names of birds, animals, herbs and trees." Likewise, in the *Lunyu*, Confucius recommended that "He who wants to be a scholarly person, should read poetry in order to develop in himself a soul oriented to truth and beauty. Then, read the Moral Laws in order to stay on the true path, and then learn music to be able to harmonically ensoul himself."

Between Confucius' highest idea of the intellectually, morally, and aesthetically educated person, the *junzi*, and Schiller's concept of the beautiful soul, there exists an intimate inner connection. In *Grace and Dignity*, Schiller writes, "We call it a beautiful soul when the moral sentiment has assured itself of all emotions of a person, ultimately to the degree that it may abandon the guidance of the will to emotions, and never run the danger of being in contradiction with its own decisions. Hence, in a beautiful soul, individual deeds are not properly moral, rather, the entire character is. And further, it is in such a beautiful soul that sensuousness and reason, duty and inclination, harmonize; and grace is its epiphany." In Confucius he says, "This person can follow the wishes of his heart without infringing on proportion."

For Confucius, this development of the individual up to the highest ideal of the intellectual, moral, and aesthetically educated person, the *junzi* the noble person, was the precondition for a well-structured state. "When the personality is well educated, only then the home is administered. When the home is administered, then the state can be ordered. When the state is ordered, only then can we have world peace. Once humanity is in order, thus will also Heaven and Earth and the whole procession of nature come to order: All disruptions of the course of nature are but the result of disorder among men and the faulty development of character in the ruler."

Exactly in the same way, Schiller drew the conclusion from the failure of the French Revolution caused by the Jacobin terror, that a great historical moment had found a little people, where the objective potential for transformation existed, but the subjective, moral precondition was missing. "From now on," Schiller said, "any improvement in the political realm can only happen through the ennoblement of the individual." For him, this is also the precondition for the well-being of the state. In the Fourth Aesthetical Letter, he says, "Every individual man, one can say, carries by predisposition, a purely ideal man within himself—to agree with those whose immutable unity, in all his outer alterations, is the great task of his existence. This pure man, who gives himself to be recognized more or less distinctly, in every subject, is represented through the state." And Schiller adds, "This congruence should not come to pass in that the state represses the individual, but that the individual becomes the state. And that man, in time, ennobles himself to the man in the idea."

The Future in the Present

It is also clearly the idea of a more perfect future which guides actions in the present. This clear vision also gives the criteria for making an educated prognosis of the future. Confucius says on this, "The path to the highest truth leads to clearly recognizing the future." In the book *Proportion and Mean—Zhongyong*, he speaks of the duty of man to search for truth as "Who seeks truth, chooses the good and stays with it." The path of the highest truth makes it possible that man can recognize in advance if a kingdom is about to flourish—then there are favorable signs; or if a kingdom is about to collapse, then there are ominous signs.

Nicholas of Cusa, who founded modern natural science with his new scientific method of thinking at the level of the coincidence of opposites, *Coincidentia Oppositorum*—the "win-win" thinking of the 15th Century—was also the inventor of precise scientific measurement, and made the decisive step in formulating a representative system of the nation-state. He is—prior to Schiller—the philosopher who had the greatest affinity to Confucius. He had the same idea that the sage can recognize the future on the basis of the recapitulation of the overall development of the universe to his time, through prior knowledge in his mind of that which he seeks. Without prior knowledge, one does not know either what is the proper question, nor if what is found is really what was sought. For Schiller, too, the inner-educated ideal of a better future is that in which man acts on reality, in that he gives direction toward the good. In the "Ninth Aesthetical Letter," he demands that this idea must be fully educated in the heart so that the idea can effectively confront the dubious society of reality. He says, "Live with the century, but be not its creature. Give the contemporaries what they need, not what they praise." With this, Schiller demands the same inner moral independence as Confucius, which can only be achieved with a completely human education of the character.

In such matters, the intent is not merely to realize in one's self the highest ideas, but to actively contribute to the betterment of society. Likewise, true knowledge is not won by mere contemplative observation, but by active transformation of society. Confucius says in his book *The Great Learning—Daxue*, "The highest knowledge is that reality is impacted; Only when it engages has reality reached its height. Then ideas become true. When the ideas are true, only then is the consciousness just. Only when the consciousness is just, will the person be educated. Only if the person is educated, is the home regulated and the state governed, and is there peace in the world."

With Nicholas of Cusa, the same idea is expressed in this way: That "only when all microcosms are developing in the best possible way, can harmony in the macrocosm come into being." At the same time, this development is not static, as the further education of one, engages like a fugal counterpoint in the development of the other, and leads to a harmonic development of the totality. Such Cusa-like thinking, albeit in a Confucian way, emerges from the words of Chinese Foreign Minister Wang Yi, when he says, "The Belt and Road Initiative is no Chinese solo act, but a symphony performed by all nations."

Schiller, in his later years, occupied himself with the question of how the resolution of inner conflicts, both in the single individual, as in society, could be portrayed in poetry and whereby "the voluntary unification of inclinations with the law, the pinnacle of moral dignity to a more refined nature, is nothing less than the idea of beauty applied to the real world." He depicts here the idea that reality should strive for, in the sense of Percy Shelley, that "poets are the unacknowledged legislators of the world."

The Coming Adulthood of Mankind

Why should it not be conceivable that mankind becomes adult? That we cease to attack each other like uneducated four-year-olds? Or, to express it otherwise, why arrest the development of humanity in senseless geopolitical conflicts? Why should it not be within our immediate grasp to eliminate poverty from this world? To make possible universal education for all children? With that, making the beautiful soul the goal of education, as Wilhelm von Humboldt did, but also Confucius. The most crucial question for Confucius and Schiller was educating love of mankind, which Confucius valued higher than life itself, more important than fire and water, and which Schiller called "the most beautiful phenomena in the soul-filled creation; the omnipotent magnet in the spiritual world, the source of devotion, and the most sublime virtue, where man becomes richer with everything he loves." For Confucius, the love of mankind was the highest morality; making possible all other ethical values, as in the *Lunyu* [*Analects*], where Confucius says, "All deeds of man must be embodied in it; otherwise, they are worthless."

From this, it also follows that man must have compassion for the other. For Lessing, the most compassionate human being was also the best, "as he is ready to act on the foundation of all civil virtues and demonstrates all manners of generosity." It is told that Confucius never satisfied his hunger when eating next to a man in mourning, as he did not want to enjoy his meal when another one suffered. Likewise, in the *Lunyu*, Confucius emphasizes how important it is for a state to continuously cultivate in its citizens a love of mankind. Otherwise, it is doomed. Confucius said, "To lead a people lacking education into war, is to guarantee their doom." The analogy for the present is obvious, and requires no comment.

Both Confucius and Schiller advocated cultivation of the individual and society by means of aesthetical education, whereby art—which itself must attain the highest standard—plays the most important role. Schiller demanded from poets, as from artists generally, to elevate themselves "to the highest moral and aesthetical height before practicing their art. The task of enno-

Dawei Dong/Asian Cultural Institute

Musicians perform traditional Chinese songs for stringed instruments, the ehru and the guzheng, at the April 14 concert sponsored by the Foundation for the Revival of Classical Culture.

bling that personality to the highest degree, of refining it into the purest, most splendid humanity, is the first and most important business the artist must address before he may venture to move his audience. There can be no greater value to his poetry than that it is a perfected imprint of a truly interesting disposition of a truly interesting perfected mind."

In his poem "The Artists," Schiller assigns artists the responsibility for civilization. "The dignity of man into your hands is given. Its keeper be. It sinks with you; with you it will be risen." The same idea is found in Confucius, in particular regarding music. He says, "Music rises from the heart. When the emotions are touched, they are expressed in sound. And when the sounds take definite forms, we have music. Therefore, the music of a peaceful and prosperous country is quiet and joyous, and the government is orderly. The music of a country in turmoil shows dissatisfaction and anger, and the government is chaotic. The music of a destroyed country shows sorrow and remembrance of the past, and the people are distressed. Thus, we see music and government are directly connected to one another." In a very beautiful treatise on music, Confucius writes, "When the likes and dislikes are not properly controlled, and our conscious minds are distracted by the material world, we lose our true selves and the principle of reason, and nature is destroyed. When man is constantly exposed to things in the material world which affect him, and does not control his likes and dislikes, then he becomes overwhelmed by material reality. He becomes dehumanized and materialistic. When a man becomes dehumanized or materialistic, the principle of reason in nature is destroyed, and man is submerged in his own desires. From this arises rebellion, disobedience, cunning and deceit, and general immorality. We have then a picture of the strong bullying the weak; the majority persecuting the minority; the clever one deceiving the simple-minded; the physically strong going for violence; the sick and crippled not being taken care of; and the aged and young helpless, and not cared for. This is the way of chaos."

One Universal Principle

So music, he says, is connected with the principles of human conduct. "Therefore, animals know sound, but they do not know tones. He who understands music comes very near to the understanding of the *li*"—the *li* meaning to find one's proper place in the state and in the universe. "If a man has mastered both the *li* and music, we call him virtuous because virtue is the mastery of fulfillment. Truly great music shares the principle of harmony with the universe. When the soil is poor, things do not grow. When the fishing is not regulated according to the seasons, the fishes and the turtles do not mature. When the climate deteriorates, animal and plant life degenerates. When the world is chaotic, the rituals and the music become licentious. We find a type of music that is rueful without restraint, and joyous without calm. Therefore, the superior man tries to create harmony in the human heart by the rediscovery of human nature, and tries to promote music as the means to the perfection of human culture. When such music prevails and people's minds are led toward the right ideals and aspirations, we may see the appearance of a great nation. Character is the backbone of our human nature, and music is the flowering of character."

How can it be that between a philosopher from China who lived almost 2,500 years ago, and a German poet who was active 200 years ago, we find such a similarity of ideas and methods? Naturally, Schiller knew Confucius; he dedicated to him the poem "The Sayings of Confucius," which ended with the lines: "Relentless, forward you must strive; never tired, standing still. If thou wilt see perfection, it must unfold in breadth. Shall the world shape you? In the depths you must rise; let Nature show itself to you. Only perseverance leads to the goal; only fulfilledness leads to clarity. And in the abyss lives the truth."

The inner affinity between Confucius and Schiller is because both are inspired by the same idea of sublime humanity, in which they were deeply convinced would be achievable in the future as the true identity of mankind, despite intermittent setbacks. Already 100 years earlier, Leibniz, taking note of the fact that the Emperor Kangxi came to similar mathematical results, drew the conclusion that there must be a universally knowable principle, and more generally recognized that this affinity between Chinese and European culture exists. He wrote, "By a unique decision of destiny, as I believe, it is so that the highest civilization and the highest technical civilization of mankind are now collected, as it were, at the two extremes of our continent. In Europe and China, which like a Europe of the East, adorns the opposite end of the Earth. Perhaps the highest providence pursues the goal by which the most civilized, and at the same time most distant peoples, are reaching out their arms; and gradually leads all found between them to life filled by reason."

Unfortunately, Europe today does not keep up with these high points, but is instead turning to, in the words of Lavrov, "post-Christian values." To the contrary, the Confucian tradition is experiencing a great renaissance in China right now, led by President Xi Jinping, who has made it a point that Confucian teaching must be taught on all levels of society. We could turn back to the European high tradition at will. We could go back to Plato, the Classical Greeks, the Italian Renaissance, the German Classical period. And this is the European culture which is the New Paradigm of the New Silk Road, and if it is revived with a dialogue of culture with it, then at any time we can make it alive and with it a new Renaissance. If each nation and each culture makes alive again their highest cultural achievements, presenting to themselves and other nations their best aspect, it is certain a new renaissance will come—seizing upon the best from universal history, but beyond that, enthusiastically creating new corresponding concepts for mankind achieving maturity. We should remember that it was Benjamin Franklin who was inspired by Confucius' moral teachings, to shape the young America. So, there is an absolute basis for this dialogue.

Schiller foresaw: "No one be like the other; be each like to the highest. How to achieve that? Each one be, in his person, complete."

The Coming Polyphony of East and West

by Dr. Patrick Ho

Dr. Patrick Ho, co-chairman of the China Energy Fund Committee and author of the Belt and Road Monograph 2016, *delivered the following, slightly abridged remarks, entitled "The Belt and Road Initiative—and Corresponding Ideas in Chinese and Western Philosophy," to a Schiller Institute conference in New York City on April 14, 2017. His remarks followed the opening presentation to the* Dialogue of Civilizations *panel by Helga Zepp-LaRouche on the second day of the conference.*

Good morning, everybody. Mme. Helga Zepp-LaRouche, distinguished guests, ladies and gentlemen, it warms my heart to see, on a Friday morning, this day of Good Friday, that there are still so many of you here to learn about Chinese culture. It's really fantastic.

We are here today to discuss how Chinese metaphysics has influenced the rest of the world. We will learn from history while also keeping the future in mind.

What is China? What is it that has held so many people together for millennia? What is "Chineseness"? What gives the Chinese the sense of what it is to be Chinese? Well, all you have to remember is three things: China is land. China is people. China is civilization.

China, the most populated country, has 56 races, each with a varying set of customs, habits, and living conditions. China is extremely diverse, very pluralistic, and very much decentralized. They are held together by a common written language and a set of cultural core values derived from millennia of cultural legacies and civilization.

China is indeed in so many ways not like the West. It's not primarily even a nation state where its people are defined by a political identity, but a *civilization state*, where its people are defined by a cultural identity. This helps explain why the Chinese place such a huge emphasis on unity and stability, the basis for the state and the distinctive notion of family and social relations, and why they embrace ideas such as "harmony with diversity." And unlike Europe, China never sought to acquire overseas colonies.

The Chinese state bears a fundamentally different relationship to society compared with any Western state. In China, the state, or the government, is seen as intimate, as a member of the family, a necessary good, rather than as in the Western discourse, a problem, a threat, or even an enemy of the people. For Chinese, the state is the embodiment of the civilization as such: Its legitimacy comes from the cultural legacy and core values that it upholds and protects. So the legacy and legitimacy of the authority of the Chinese government does not come from the people. It comes from Heaven. And I'll explain what Heaven is all about. Heaven means *morality*. So, it is ethics, it is morals, that give the government its right to govern.

EIRNS/Jason Ross

Dr. Patrick Ho

A Second, Global Renaissance

Rather than fear what lies ahead, we Chinese are aspiring to a new and peaceful world civilization, based on principles of benevolence, respect, trust, equality, and continuing human advancement. This vision, driven by humanity's historic longing for peace and prosperity, is renewed by our appreciation that all of us on this Earth of ours share a common destiny, which each and every one of us has the responsibility to defend and to safeguard.

In many ways we can already see how the return of China to prominence has not only been good for China, but also good for the world. Economic: By lifting hundreds of millions of people out of poverty, China has contributed to global prosperity. Philosophical: China's most significant contribution to the world will be intangible—its cultural wisdom, its metaphysics, its outlook on life and on the Universe, and its traditional values, a resource unique to China, rare gems formed by heat and pressure over immense periods of time. Few if any countries can claim the cultural longevity of China, and China's culture is vast and its traditions run deep. Indeed, it is the only one of the four ancient civilizations that has not been interrupted and is still in existence.

The re-emergence of Chinese culture will therefore help bring balance to global culture. The propagation and exchange will lead to a wiser, more thoughtful, and more creative global culture. As it has in the past, exchange will spur innovation and creativity, and cause a flourishing in science, arts, and humanities. It will lead to a second, global Renaissance.

The *Dao* and Sustainable Development

Let's go into a very important Chinese contribution to modern literature: the *Dao De Jing* by Laozi. It is considered the bible of Daoism. It's the book of profound wisdom and great learning, and it is the book that has been translated in the most versions second only to the Bible. *Dao De Jing*, together with *Yi Jing* [*I Ching*], provides the architectural framework for Chinese metaphysics and an indigenous religion.

The *Dao De Jing* has a long and complex textual history. Versions and commentaries date back two millennia, including ancient bamboo, silk, and paper manuscripts discovered in the 20th Century. The oldest discovered portion dates back to the late 4th Century B.C.E.

The received *Dao De Jing* is a short text of just 5,000 Chinese characters in 81 brief sentences. It has two parts, the *Tao Jing* and the *De Jing*.

There are many possible translations of the book's title. *Dao* or *tao* is the pivotal and defined term in ancient Chinese thought. The common translation is "The Way." You all know what is "The Way." You read in the *Gospel According to St. John*: "He is the Way." "Way" resists definition in English. We can do very little more than just offer mere synonyms that are neither as familiar nor as broad in application. Typically, we would use "way" to explain terms such as "course, method, the manner, mode, means, practice, fashion, technique," and so on.

In Chinese the character *dao* is part of the doctrine or truth or principle or law, and of course, ethics, reason, religious, orthodoxy, thank, apologize, tell, explain, inform, and so on. These are all *dao*.

A more concrete translation of *dao* is the "the road" or "the path." Throughout Classical texts *dao*s are spoken, heard, forgotten, transmitted, learned, studied, understood, misunderstood, distorted, mastered, and performed with pleasure. Different countries in historical periods have different *dao*.

This term, however, has special meaning within the context of Taoism, where it implies the essential, unnamable process of the Universe. *Dao* really means the entire Universe. A lot of people say *dao* is a Supreme Being. Whether it is a Supreme Being or not, nobody knows. It is that thing that runs everything.

So the first line of *Dao De Jing* is, "The *dao* that can be described is not the true *dao*. The true *dao* cannot be described or comprehended by humans. It is so vast, so superlative, so magnificent, it is beyond our imagination, beyond human description, beyond words, and beyond comprehension."

So *dao* means virtue, personal character, inner strength, virtuosity, integrity, and so on. The semantics for this Chinese word resembles English "virtue," which developed from the Italian *virtù*, an archaic sense of inner potency or divine power, as in the healing virtue of a drug, to the modern meaning of moral excellence or goodness.

Combined with the compound word *dao de*, the meaning of *jing* is canon or great book or classic, but *dao* means the virtue of the system itself. *De* is the implementation of this virtue, it's how we embody this virtue, how we live up to this virtue. So *de* is a way of living, it's something we can practice, something that can be seen and felt, whereas *dao* is something to aspire to and not to be known. Thus *Dao De Jing* can be translated as *The Classic of the Way's Vir-*

tues or *The Book of the Way of Virtue*.

Work has been underway to apply the wisdom of *Dao De Jing* in addressing modern-day problems and difficulties in life. The book may yield clues to a sustainable lifestyle, which is paramount in underpinning all initiatives leading to reaching the 17 targets of the 2030 Sustainable Development Goals rolled out by the United Nations.

We must inspire responsibility in those who are affluent. We should live in a sustainable lifestyle; that is: use what you need but not what you want, because what you want, what you desire is limitless, it has no meaning. Human desire sees no satiety, it cannot be satisfied. We should be careful in consumption—use resources efficiently, sparingly, responsibly, and be smart—and oppose excess and extravagance.

Statue of Confucius at Confucian Temple in Shanghai, China.

Eastern and Western Core Values

Let us now go into the crux of how East and West cultural core values can blend together.

The Renaissance brought humanism into a European society previously dominated by the Church. But whereas Western humanism centers on the self or individual and emphasizes individualism and other specific values, Eastern humanism not only focuses on the human relationship, which thereby prescribes the essence of the Chinese person, but on the entire holistic makeup in which humanity is part and parcel of the overall arrangement.

Chinese culture is dominated by Confucianism, which centers its principles on the ancient religious foundation of Daoism. While establishing the social values and ideals for the traditional society, Confucian philosophy presupposes three biospheres of human interactions: Heaven, Earth, and Humans. And man must find peace in all three biospheres.

For the Man-Man biosphere, Confucius emphasized proper conduct in one's social relations, because it is in the company of others that man reaches his ultimate

fulfillment. This code of behavior is called *li*, which Mme. Helga just referred to, the social and ethical norms that guide people to do the appropriate things at the right time, in the right place, manifesting respect and kindness. It's something like etiquette.

The most important of all virtues is benevolence, *ren*, which is love of fellow humans, a sense of compassion based on the dignity of human life and great self-respect. We cultivate *ren* by putting ourselves in the position of others, and treating them as you wish them to treat you. Confucius said, "Do not do to others what you would not like others to do unto you." And "Do unto others what you want others to do unto you." So benevolence means the practice of these two golden principles, which not only can be found in the Chinese literature of Confucianism, but also in the Bible, in the Quran, and in sacred texts of almost all religions. And these two golden principles have a universality that permeates all world ethical, cultural, and religious traditions throughout the ages.

Regarding Man-Earth interactions: We are ultimately linked to all life on Earth, and therefore must treat our environment with respect and care. Man's obsession with development and growth—and particularly still more things to give us greater convenience, pleasure, and comfort—contradicts all teachings against extreme greed and the principle calling for moderation. Whereas Western civilization often regards nature as an object for eventual conquest, the Chinese treat nature with great reverence and respect. Chinese are appreciative of nature, because humans and Earth, as part of nature, are deemed to be one entity. Such a world outlook raises up a civilization with a sense of tolerance in pursuit of coexistence and harmony. A pinnacle achievement in life is to be One with Heaven.

It is because of Confucius' teaching that the primary concern is humanity and the interrelationship between people; Confucianism has only a general description or mention of Heaven or God, leaving a large amount of room in the spiritual realm for Chinese people to learn from the other civilizations and religions, such as Buddhism from India, Islam from the Middle East, Christianity from the West.

And perhaps for that reason Chinese culture, and thus religion, is a very tolerant one, being a culture and religion of infinite possibilities and capable of accommodating all and any Supreme Beings. Chinese will seldom engage themselves in arguments about whose God is the true God and whose isn't one, or whose is a better God. Chinese, unlike other cultures of monotheism, do not have the burden of being self-ordained missionaries, defending one religion by attempting to convert everybody else to a particular religion. Perhaps Chinese regard Heaven or God as so supreme and magnificent that it is beyond description and definition by humanity, and unlimited possibilities and imagination exist with this Heavenly statement in mind.

Instead, Chinese focus on the interfacing layer between the spiritual sphere and the material world, which can be explained as a network of social and interpersonal relationships between man and his inner self, man and his surrounding environment, and man and his fellow men.

Therefore, any type of belief or religion can easily blend into the Chinese spiritual world. But for it to be practiced by the people in the local communities, it has to be filtered through the Confucian network of traditional and social relationships and be "Sinicized," or interpreted with Chinese characteristics. Therefore, when Buddhism, Islam, Christianity, or Judaism was introduced into China, it was customized with local interpretations and was blended in with the domestic practices of Chinese society.

A 'Heart-Centered,' Harmonious World

From a material-life-dominated world to a heart-centered, harmonious world, change is itself eternal. That is what the book *Yi Jing* told us.

Some analysts believe that a large number of social problems emerged because of the collapse of traditional values and a lack of spiritual life. To write a prescription for contemporary society, one has to review the development of human civilization and the social value system. And a "heart culture" of Confucianism is the right way to solve these problems.

The process of human development might be broadly divided into four stages, both individually and collectively as the whole of humanity is concerned. The four stages are material needs, spiritual needs, individual needs, and collective needs or altruism.

In the earlier stage of society, humans pursued the improvement of material life and the establishment of a property system as the ultimate goals. These goals met the physiological and safety needs at the lowest level of existence in the hierarchies of need. In the material-dominated agricultural society, the core values were industriousness, thriftiness, simplicity, honesty, and adherence to the law.

After having solved the problems of food, clothing, and safety, humans began to think about the next level of requirements and needs and demands, which is social—asking for love and belonging and esteem, asking for self-respect. The theocratic system in medieval Europe and the Chinese imperial system of the Zhou Dynasty both formed feudal societies which believed in God and Heaven. But the core values of this period emphasized hierarchy, worship of Heaven and ancestors, loyalty, filial piety, and righteousness.

Renaissance Individualism

The Renaissance removed the shroud of theocratic gloom over Europe, emancipated the mind, called for freedom, inspired creativity, and enlightened the next generations. It also translated the God-worship culture into a human exploration culture. These represented a human turn to a higher level of needs, of self-actualization through individualism. This culture, encouraging subjective innovations and calling for individual freedom, achieved the release of humanity, accelerated the emergence of capitalism, laid a foundation for science, and established the rule of law. It also introduced individualism into philosophy, shaped the modern, people-oriented society, and generated the modern ideas of freedom, democracy, human rights, the rule of law, equality, and fraternity.

Humanism, however, was distorted by individual desire. The absence of constraint from traditional religions and moralities ultimately led to the alienation of human nature.

To solve the problem of today's society, it is not enough to depend only on what the West has achieved. We need to move from the individualistic, people-oriented human culture, to an altruistic, heart-centered human culture. Since ancient times, "heart culture"—loosely interpreted as *ren*, or in Greek the word is *agapē*, broad love, unconditional love—has occupied an important position in Chinese culture, one that plays a key role in keeping Chinese culture different from Western culture.

Confucius said that "one needs to cultivate individual moral character—keep the family in order, run the country well, and bring peace to the world, but first and foremost, one needs to rectify the heart." That also means to purify the heart. To rectify the heart means you have to set your heart right and proper.

Xunzi said, "The heart decides one's Being."

Dong Zhongshu, another scholar, said, "The heart is essential to one's body."

Zhu Xi said, "The heart dominates."

Wang Chuanshan said, "In one's body, the heart is before everything."

Wang Shou-ren said, "People are the heart of the Universe and the heart is the lord of the Universe."

The "heart" in Chinese is a collective consciousness and is frequently taken to mean the "soul," the interconnection among human beings that connect one human being with another, and with nature and with the ultimate being itself.

Conscience, which is the heavenly principle, already exists in one's heart. As long as one is trying hard to cultivate the heart, conscience will not be blinded by lust, and will finally achieve the unison of knowing and doing. And these indicate that the heart rules the relationship between the body and the mind.

How East and West Come Together

The world is now slowly transitioning from a competition of hard power to a contest of soft power, Confucianism's teaching that tolerance fosters greatness is a means to hold the world together with virtue, and its long historical heritage of heart culture is the cultural fountainhead of Chinese soft power. The Chinese understand peace as something internal. It starts within every one of us and should be cultivated and nurtured. Before undertaking such a pursuit, we must first set our minds in order and then ensure that our purpose is sincere, so that our quest for wisdom can become complete through a careful discernment of nature. Thus, wisdom is achieved.

Acquiring real self-discipline will yield harmony within the family, paving the way to good governance and global peace. This is Confucius' utopian vision of peace. Peace on Earth begins with finding the inner peace inherent in every one of us. We must be at peace with ourselves before we can be at peace with one another. Peace comes from within, not from yonder. For peace to prevail on Earth, let peace first prevail in us, in our hearts.

So let us find peace by loving one another as we love ourselves, and by respecting and loving one another's country, as we respect and love our own country. Chinese traditional cultural core values are established and time-tested while undergoing twists and turns throughout history. These values are modified and adapted to different times and contexts, and yet are made applicable to solving the problems of the present time. In different eras and locations, the manifestations and application methods could vary, but the underlying core values and principles remain steadfast and sustained.

Ever since the mid-19th Century, the Chinese people have been looking forward to a modernized China with a Renaissance of Chinese culture. We believe that the values of East and West are not incompatible. Instead they constitute a set of values at two ends of the spectrum, just like the *yin* and *yang* of *T'ai Chi*. A combination of Chinese and Western cultures and Chinese modernization will lead to a second Renaissance of humanity. Western and Eastern emphases of core values appear to define the latitude of interpretation: Individual with Community; Rights with Obligations; Freedom with Responsibilities; Achievements with Sacrifices and Commitments; Competition with Alliances; and Diversity with Harmony. The two sets of values operate with one another as two opposing principles in nature, complementing and supplementing one another.

The Polyphony of *He*

By combining the strength of the East and the West we can make possible a multipolar world order for the modern century, and achieve the ultimate Chinese core value of *He*, meaning "harmony." *He* means peace, calm, sum and summation; a draw, meaning no winners, no losers—mix and blend so as to become indistinguishable one from the other. It is also a process of achieving commonality in the face of diversity. All the different elements, each with its own characteristics, work together for a common cause, and in the end the synergy produces a new collective energy that surpasses the glory and splendor of its parts in sum total.

Through this very powerful process of *He*, Chinese culture has been able to assimilate all the different cultures of its foreign invaders and conquerors, ultimately rising over them with a superior and richer and more forgiving system. And *He* is indeed the central pillar of Chinese soft power in its core value. *He* means harmony. As Helga just said earlier, what is harmony? If everybody is singing the same tune, it is not harmony, it's called unison. If everybody sings the same notes, plays the same instrument, produces the same melody, that's not *He*, that's unison. That's everybody becoming the same. It's not interesting.

What is polyphony? Polyphony means there's har-monization—everybody playing a different tune, everybody playing a different note, but together it sounds beautiful! That's harmony. It's everybody playing a different tune, but yet, all those different tunes conform to a certain mode of thinking, meaning everybody plays to the conductor's baton. If everyone plays a different tune, and at different times, and in different places, it would not be harmony; it has to be orchestrated, differently, but the same. That is called harmony.

Therefore, this Renaissance of Chinese culture is not simply for China or the Chinese nation. New elements will be injected into global civilization, paving the way for a second Renaissance, for the entire human race. This second Renaissance brings about a new dimension to define an awakened generation of humanity.

Helga Zepp-LaRouche in Dialogue With Dr. Patrick Ho

The following brief dialogue between Patrick Ho and Helga Zepp-LaRouche immediately followed Dr. Ho's presentation on April 14.

Helga Zepp-LaRouche: Thank you very much, Dr. Ho. Patrick, I think this was very enlightening. I think you have given us a very rich picture. I have only one observation to make. The reason I suggested this conference in the first place was—I think that you, when you say "Western Civilization," are referring to the way Western Civilization is today, whereas I was trying to say that there are these two traditions, the oligarchical tradition and what I call the republican tradition for the common good. And I think it is very important to somehow make that distinction, because we want to reject the values of this present system. If you just say "Western Civilization," it doesn't do justice.

Patrick Ho: Helga, you are absolutely right, because nowadays what is generally meant by "modernization," is actually "westernization." A lot of people in the East take the two terms to be equivalent to one another, meaning modernization is westernization, and that is the only way of getting modernized, which is not

true. But at the same time we should not reject westernization as throwing out the baby with the bathwater. There is something good in it, and what we really need is to combine the eastern virtues with the western virtues and come up with something that can transcend both of them and rise up and be better than the two put together in summation.

There is a lot of room where we can learn from one another, and I think, in the future we will be seeing one trend, because for the last two hundred years the world has been dominated by a small fraction of human civilization—that is Europe and North America combined. But now, with the emerging economies and the emerging powers from the developing nations in the East, from China, from India, from Brazil, the Middle East countries, ASEAN countries, African countries—we'll be hearing more and more about civilizations that we have not paid any attention to before, and we'll be learning more and more about the needs, the requirements, and the aspirations of other peoples that we have never known to have existed before, have not listened to before, have not paid any attention to before— but they will be playing a more and more important role. As a humanist, I welcome this change. This is the

EIRNS/Jason Ross

Dr. Patrick Ho and Helga Zepp-LaRouche, April 14, 2017.

ultimate democratization of—humanization of—humanity, and is the platform of the world which is a shared future of humanity, because ultimately we are in the same boat. We share a common destiny. There is only one planet; that is planet earth. There is no planet B.

Following a question from the audience as to the nature of the oligarchy, a further exchange took place:

Zepp-LaRouche: Thank you for that, because I think . . . in Western history, up until the Fifteenth Century, there was nothing but oligarchy. You always had a small elite trying to keep the people backward, trying to exploit their privileges, and when the German philosopher Nicholas of Cusa emerged, he was the first one to develop the idea of the representative system, and the idea that the state was devoted to the common good.

In France at that point, you had Louis XI: During his twenty-year reign the living standard of the population doubled, and you had the beginning of the modern nation-state, which had the idea that you need science and technology to improve the living conditions of the people. Since the Fifteenth Century in Europe you always had a back and forth, where sometimes you had a government which was for the common good. In the recent period I would say Adenauer and de Gaulle were mild expressions of that tendency. You had backlashes

like Nixon, where, despite the fact that he opened the door to China, he was a terrible step back, because he tried to undo the Civil Rights movement—he was going back to the Confederacy.

So you had these struggles, and you could always measure very clearly whether government is devoted to the progress of civilization, or does it represent the oligarchical system. With these went also very clear philosophers, thinkers, and scientists, and there was a struggle over these ideas.

To Dr. Ho: Maybe some other time we will be able to get into the depths of this, but my modest understanding was always that Daoism was more linked to the backward tendencies in European history, and also the idea of complacency, to merely concentrating on one's own internal development. That's why I always thought that Confucius is really, absolutely the corresponding figure to Plato, to Cusa, to Leibniz, and to Schiller.

I think that if we want to get out of this crisis, then we need to develop a more active dialogue among these positive traditions, *and then move to the future*—joint space exploration, going to a completely different way—because we must define the present from the standpoint of the future, if we are going to find solutions. Obviously you cannot exhaust this, but I think this is the kind of dialogue we should deepen.

Dr. Ho: We'll do that next time!

Zepp-LaRouche: Okay!

DR. DAVE WANG

Confucius and Benjamin Franklin

Summary of Dr. Dave Wang's remarks to the second day of the conference on April 14. Dr. Wang is the managing librarian of the Queens Library at Laurelton, in Queens, New York City, and Adjunct Professor, St. Johns University.

Good afternoon. I, like everybody here, enjoyed Dr. Patrick Ho's presentation. I learned a lot of about Chinese culture and the new initiative the Chinese have started.

Before I start my presentation, I should express my appreciation to Bill Jones, and to John and Renée Sigerson from the Schiller Institute, who made this presentation possible. I don't think I can really do a thorough presentation of my research. I will briefly introduce you to my publications on Chinese cultural influences on the United States.[1]

In one of my early papers about the Chinese cultural influence on the United States, I said that we talk about the American Dream. The American Dream started with China. Even before the colonists landed, Chinese influence had begun. Because the Virginia Company supported the exploration of North America, the company had to choose where to place the landing. It wanted to land somewhere close to a place from which it could get to China!

France supported the American Revolution. Why? The French didn't believe that George Washington's guerrillas could win the War of Independence without international support, basically from France. One of the main reasons France supported the war, was that it didn't want the British to monopolize the opportunity to trade with China.

Benjamin Franklin used the idea of China's Great Wall in the French and Indian War (1754-1763),[2] Frank-

Dr. Dave Wang

EIRNS/Jason Ross

lin thought we should build a wall, like the Chinese wall, to protect the United States. He mentioned this wall twice, once in the French and Indian War, and again in the Revolutionary War. It's obvious this wall would protect the newborn United States.

I wrote about Benjamin Franklin and Confucian moral philosophy, and that Franklin used the principles of Confucius to cultivate his virtue. In 2011, I published "The U.S. Founders and China: The Origin of Chinese Cultural Influence on the United States," which includes a picture of the Supreme Court Building, and there is Confucius right there. When you go to the United States Supreme Court, if you go to the east gate, you can see Confucius right there.

Franklin published an essay on the morals of Confucius in 1737 in his *Pennsylvania Gazette*. He published several chapters of Confucius' moral philosophy in 1737. In a 1747 letter to George Whitefield, a very well-known pastor, Franklin wrote, "Confucius was my example. I followed Confucius." Twelve years later, Franklin published Confucius' works.

In 1784, after the Revolution, some veterans hoped they could hand down their glories, their titles, to their descendants. They organized the Cincinnatus Society for this purpose. Franklin was not happy about the idea of handing down your title, your glory, to the next generation—that's the inheritance system, or the aristocratic system of the Europeans, which was just what our Revolution opposed. What's the meaning of the Revolution, if we restore the European aristocratic inheritance system? That's totally wrong. We should adopt the Chinese merit system, and people with talents will be selected to serve the public.

Naturally not all scholars agree with my conclusions. Professor David Weir of Cooper Union published a book in 2011 in which, in part, he did agree. He said indeed, Benjamin Franklin learned a lot from Chinese culture, especially from Confucius' philosophy. However, he

1. See Dr. Wang's weblog at http://foundingfathersandchina.blogspot.com/

2. "Defending the American Colonies: Benjamin Franklin's Great Wall, 1756-1776," *Virginia Review of Asian Studies*, Vol. 17 (2015), pp. 213-220.

said, the influence of Confucius' ideas suddenly stopped. After the Revolution, there was no more Confucian influence.

I thought, that's not right. So I wrote a lengthy paper to him about Confucius in the founding of America and discussed how the Founding Fathers—Benjamin Franklin, Thomas Jefferson, and the others—tried to build a new virtue with the new nation. They thought Confucius' ideas would be good—that we can use those ideas to build a new virtue. So we cannot continue our old virtue.

I discuss the journey of the United States to adopting the merit system in the selection of government officials in a paper I finished several days ago, "A Journey of Adapting the Confucian Merit System from Benjamin Franklin to the Pendleton Act of 1883." Since I work in a public library, one of my tasks is to provide materials for my customers to prepare for the civil service examination, in order to get a government jobs. And that's an idea from China. Franklin mentioned it in 1784. But his proposal wasn't adopted then. Why not?

In 1881, President James Garfield was assassinated by a job-seeker, Charles Guiteau. Why did he kill him? Because he thought he should have gotten a public job. He had supported Garfield's election and he had made a great contribution to Garfield's victory. At that time, from Thomas Jefferson until James Garfield, the United States system for selecting government employees was the "spoils system." Under the spoils system, anyone who made a contribution to the victory of a political candidate would get a government job—all my friends, all my relatives, get government jobs.

And then, the public decided, "We've got to stop it. We cannot do this any more." We've got to get Franklin's idea back; we have to select public officials through the merit system. Everyone has to pass a public civil service examination. Now there are about 4.5 million public employees in the United States; 80% had to pass civil service examinations. For the United States to adopt this system, it took a century, from Franklin in 1784 to 1884, one hundred years, to pass the Pendleton Act, to make the merit system official.

I'll conclude by reading something by the late Dr.

THE

Pennsylvania *GAZETTE.*

Containing the freshest Advice• Foreign and Domestick.

FROM MARCH 14. TO MARCH 21. 1737,8.

[Continuation of the Morals of Confucius.]

Wilton Dillon, perhaps one of the best cultural anthropologists in the world. He wrote, "The Research on China and Our Founding Fathers,"[3] in which he says:

"I met Dave Wang at an Aspen Institute meeting of Friends of Franklin. Meeting this Chinese scholar from St. John's University in New York opened up a floodgate of new insights about Chinese influence on our founding fathers and colonial North America. Prof. Wang travels the world now to share his new findings. I have given copies of some of his papers to former U.S. Senators Larry Pressler, Republican from South Dakota, and Harris Wofford, Democrat from Pennsylvania, when they lectured in China on 'the two party system.' Celebrating one nation's cultural gifts to another—and especially, the capacity to receive—makes for good diplomacy.

" 'How China Helped to Shape American Culture: The Founding Fathers and Chinese Civilization' is the title of Wang's 2010 summary of his findings, published in the *Virginia Review of Asian Studies* (2010). Confucian philosophy, tea, porcelain, wallpaper, rhubarb, soybeans, house heating, canal and ship building, ideas about reason, rocketry, and alternative medicine, were among many cultural contributions coming from China. Franklin designed a wooden wall inspired by the Great Wall to protect Philadelphia from Indians after the French and Indian War. Jefferson's architecture showed hints of Chinese design. Wang traces Chinese influence on Thomas Paine, John Bartram, Benjamin Rush, and Jedidiah Morse, among others. ...

"Lines need to be drawn between pandering for political, economic, and security goals on one hand, and historical studies of cultural contact on the other. Western, particularly U.S. influence, has helped to revolutionize Greater China. The Asian idea of *yin* and *yang* would help both interdependent parties to feel more comfortable with each other."

Thank you, everybody.
davewangnyer@gail.com

---

3. In Dillon's book, *Smithsonian Stories: Chronicle of a Golden Age, 1964-1984*, Transaction Publishers, 2015.

Renaissance and the Struggle of Ideas

This is an edited transcript of Michael Billington's April 14 address to the conference.

Dennis Speed: Our final speaker for today, the Asia Editor for *EIR*, is Mike Billington. This is a book by Mike which tells about the vacation he took [laughter], all expenses paid, by him and the Federal government: *Reflections of an American Political Prisoner* (2000), during which time he did much of the work you're about to hear.

Michael Billington: Thank you. Thank you, Dennis. "Sabbatical leave" I call it, not vacation.

I'll try, in the few minutes we have left, to answer some of the questions for which this conference was originally called, and which came up in the discussion between Helga and Patrick Ho, which are the misconceptions about Western thought in China *and* misconceptions about Confucianism in the West, and in particular, something that I did in fact do a great deal of study on while I was on my "sabbatical leave": Which is that it was precisely the British, who when they semi-colonized China, set about, as they did in all of their colonies, to profile the philosophies and cultures of those nations and pick out those backward tendencies, like the caste system in India, and define that as "the nature" of the colony, in order

Michael Billington

EIRNS/Jason Ross

keep them backward and to maintain colonial power over a divided and backward nation.

This is what happened in spades in China. And it's still very, very, much alive today, as we saw reflected in the brilliant presentation, but one which has this serious flaw, of not recognizing a misconception that persists today. Namely, that the British liberalism/imperial mentality, Darwinism and survival of the fittest, is somehow "Western thought." And I want to go through that as quickly as I can.

I think the main thing to start with is that both in the West and in China, there are not just these wonderful traditions, which Helga so beautifully drew on today, and which Patrick Ho drew on with, I think, some problems—but that these wonderful traditions that gave rise to these powerful civilizations were always battling with backward tendencies. And that wasn't discussed that much. You can understand why, but I think it's very, very important to see that, because that's the way the Empire works, to subvert—as they are now subverting—the United States. And if you, for instance, wonder how Americans could be so gullible as to believe that Russia and China are aggressive nations, that Russia is aggressive in the Ukraine and Syria; that China is aggressive in the South

Plato   Confucius

Matteo Ricci

Leibniz—Novissima Sinica

China Sea—how could you believe such foolishness? Well, it's because they've profiled America in exactly the same way, which is what we're dealing with now.

Now, in the case of Plato—and Plato and Confucius were roughly contemporaries and they're very, very similar in their recognition that it's the human mind, and the capacity to be creative and to love mankind, which characterizes man. But in the case of Plato, there was his opposite, Aristotle, who believed that man was an animal, that people were born either masters or slaves, that their mind was no better than a calculating machine, not a creative capacity to master laws of the Universe and discover new principles—but rather just a calculating machine in an Aristotelian logic. And it is this Aristotelian ideology which always guides Empire. As opposed to the Platonic, which gave rise to Renaissance thinking.

And the same thing in China: You had Confucianism, and Helga was absolutely right, I think, to raise with Patrick Ho the issue of Daoism. Confucius believed in the *Dao*, in the Way, in the principle of the Universe, but Daoism as it was developed by Laozi [Lao Tze] and Zhuangzi [Chuang Tze] was a policy which rejected creativity, which called for people to reject new technologies, in order to live with nature, to *commune* with nature, rather than to *change* nature, which is the nature of creativity.

The Jesuit Missionaries in China

And that Daoist influence was coupled with an even more evil influence, called Legalism, which was basically saying that man is an animal and can only be controlled through extremely strict government, strict laws,

strict punishment; that you had to restrain the animal instincts of men through force of arms. And this was the ideology which guided the so-called First Empire in China, and was a recurring problem through the Han Dynasty and Tang Dynasty. And there was a Renaissance in China in the Song Dynasty of the 12th Century under Zhu Xi—and Zhu Xi was one of the great minds of China, who, like Cusa and like Leibniz, basically gave a rebirth to the original concepts of Confucianism.

So these battles have gone on and on and on. And I'll say a few more things on that.

The Empire in the West—and I think I have to say this for something that comes later—has been a single Empire, from the Roman Empire through the Venetian Empire, and then into the Anglo-Dutch Empire. It moved its headquarters, but it was always the same Empire, based on the Aristotelian or bestial idea of man.

When the Jesuits first came to China, the Jesuit Matteo Ricci, whom Patrick talked about—when he and his associates first came to China, their immediate response was to see the Buddhists in their saffron robes, and to assume they were the religious leaders in China, and they immediately identified with them and began collaborating with them. And they maintained collaboration with them over time, but they quickly learned that the real religious—the real philosophers of China—were the Confucian scholars, who did not wear religious robes. This was extremely important, because in China at that time, the political leaders were the Confucian scholars. The way you became a political leader, through the merit system that Professor Wang was talking about, was that you passed examinations, which were not examinations in calculations, but they were examinations in culture, in understanding Confucius and Mencius, for example.

In poetry: You had to *be* a poet, you had to *be* a musician. You had to prove that you were truly a cultured person and therefore, had the basis upon which you could be a moral ruler.

So, they quickly then established relations with the Confucians, as Patrick also indicated—I'll come back to that.

This then led to Leibniz, who was discussed today, and who, in correspondence with the Jesuits, was reading the translations of Confucius and Mencius, and especially of Zhu Xi in the Song Dynasty. With respect to China, Leibniz recognized that the fact that China had bigger cities by far than anything in Europe, a more highly educated population than anyone in Europe, a better-organized society—to him this proved that Chinese philosophy, which he hadn't yet mastered—meant, to him that Chinese philosophy had in fact mastered the fundamental laws of man and nature, since only knowing the truth about the laws of the Universe can lead to a successful culture over the long term. This was the way Leibniz viewed this.

He published *Novissima Sinica, News from China*, based on the writings he had, mostly of Zhu Xi actually, but also of Confucius and Mencius, and was conveying the truth about China to the Europeans at that time. What Leibniz had to say about Confucianism was "it is pure Christianity, insofar as it renews the natural law inscribed in our heart"; i.e., every human being is born with this potential for truth in his heart and in his mind, and this is the Platonic idea of all men being capable of creative development, and of having a moral society.

Kang Xi, who was mentioned, the Emperor at that time, got to know the Jesuits extremely well. He mastered the Christian ideology—he didn't become a Christian; he didn't think he needed to, as Patrick was pointing out. But he believed that these truths about man and

Kang Xi

nature cohered with Confucianism, and he invited the Jesuits to go throughout the country, to spread their religion—there was no problem with this whatsoever.

The End of the Mission

I would definitely disagree with Patrick's description of how that fell apart. He said the Catholic Church decided that the Confucian rites contradicted Christian ideas and Christian rites, and therefore they broke off the connection. It didn't work that way: The Empire intervened—Venice intervened. It was the Venetians who went to work on the Vatican to stop the Popes who were collaborating with the Jesuits, and basically to coerce them— just as Trump was coerced—to go against Christian self-interests, and to declare that since Confucians honored their ancestors, this did not cohere with Christian thought—therefore you could not be both a Christian and a Confucian. But keep in mind, the Confucians were the government leaders. So, to say that Christianity was against Confucianism was to say it was against the state. And that's why Kang Xi had to say, in effect, "I can't believe this, this is absurd, but I have to throw you out." And he finally did.

And that laid the basis, just a few hundred years later, for the British to come in with their gunboats and their opium. That's how they conquered the country: They blew up its cities, and they forced them to take opium. They fought the war because the Chinese were trying to stop them from bringing opium in. So this was the beginning of the horror of the British role in China.

Now, here's where what I wanted to go through, begins. Immediately, the British picked up a bright, young scholar, named Yen Fu, who was an opium addict, which they considered very important—that he was more imaginative because he was an opium addict; they sent him off to London. And Yen Fu was trained, in depth, by the British—in Darwin, in the survival of the fittest, and especially in Herbert Spencer, who was the

Profitant de la circonstance pour engager les Chinois à se passer pour deux cent millions d'opium

person who shaped Darwinism into Social Darwinism—that man is in fact just an animal; since it's not through the creativity of the mind that man progresses, but by the strong defeating the weak: survival of the fittest.

He learned these ideas, took them back to China, and basically wrote the curriculum for all the schools that were under British direction, and taught: The British conquered us because they had wealth and power. Where did they get wealth and power? They got wealth and power by this Darwinian idea of *crushing* the weak. Being willing to crush the weak in order to be strong. We have to learn how to be Darwinian, and be strong and crush the weak. This was the attempt at total brainwashing of the Chinese population.

I would just, in passing, point out that this is exactly the way Barack Obama was brainwashed into being a killer. As he writes in his book, he suspected his stepfather had been part of the slaughter of the PKI, of the Communist Party in Indonesia, under Sukarno. Therefore, he asked him, "have you ever seen a man killed?" and his father said, "Yes, indeed, I have." He didn't admit he'd killed people—which

Yen Fu

Herbert Spencer

严复

he had; but he said, "Yes, indeed," and, "You must learn, my stepson, that there are two kinds of people: There's the strong and there's the weak, and the strong have to be willing to crush the weak. What are you going to be? Are you going to be strong or are you going to be weak?" And Obama writes about that in his book, which is where his killer instincts came from.

Here's what Yen Fu said, talking about Adam Smith's *Theory of Moral Sentiments*. He writes: "There may be those… who say that, according to [Adam] Smith's book, human morality is nothing more than a matter of self-interest and the pursuit of profit, and the principle of heaven will be lost…." He's obviously referring to the American System advocates who would argue that with such thinking, you'd lose the principle of Heaven.

"What they do not understand," Yen Fu said, "is that science concerns itself with questions of truth and falsehood, and not with whether its findings coincide with benevolence and righteousness." There's no morality in science, it's just observation—no creative thinking, it's just observation, sense-perception.

Now, just to confirm that that is what he's saying—here's what Adam Smith actually says in the *Theory of Moral Sentiments*: "Nature has directed us to the greater part of these by original and immediate instincts. Hunger, thirst, the passion which unites the two sexes, the love of pleasure, and the dread of pain, prompt us to apply those means for their own sakes, and without any consideration of their tendency to those beneficent ends which the great Director of nature intended to produce by them."

Who Was Sun Yat-Sen?

Is there any mention of the human mind in there? Pure instinct. Men are animals, no more, no less. And that is the conception which Yen Fu is defending

Sun Yat Sen

The Three Principles of the People

民族   民權   民生

People's Rule   People's Power   People's Welfare
Government of the People   Government by the People   Government for the People

NATIONALISM   DEMOCRACY   SOCIALISM

against anybody with brains, and that is what he taught to the Chinese to get them to believe it.

Now, Patrick already went through the brilliance of Sun Yat-sen and his use of Lincoln's "of the people, by the people, and for the people." Let me add, that he learned this when he was in Hawaii being trained by the Damon family, that came from Philadelphia and was part of the school of Henry Carey, whom Helga had mentioned several times—the people who promoted the Hamiltonian school. And not only did he follow Lincoln, but in his writings, in his book *The Three Principles of the People*, he explicitly talked about Alexander Hamilton, as well as John Quincy Adams and Lincoln. But he also understood the American System so well, that he polemicized against Thomas Jefferson. He said that Hamilton understood the need for industry, for infrastructure, and for the education of all people, whereas Jefferson was an agrarian fanatic, who believed in slavery and wanted to keep the country backward as an agrarian nation.

So he wrote about this, and he taught the Chinese people this. This was Sun Yat-sen bringing the American System to China.

One more thing about Sun Yat-sen—this happened during the so-called May 4th Movement, which Patrick

also mentioned. During the First World War, Sun Yat-sen polemicized against joining the British in the war against the Germans. He said, if we join the British and they win the war—and they probably will—don't think that we would share in the spoils. No. He said: We will be treated the way a farmer treats the silkworm. They will draw out the useful silk and then the worm will be used as fish food. He said, we will be used as fish food—which is exactly what happened. They joined the British—that's when Deng Xiaoping and Zhou Enlai went to France; some of you know that our presidential candidate in France, Jacques Cheminade, has been talking about that.

But after the war, the Chinese, having joined the British, were torn apart, divided up, and pieces were given to each of the imperial powers.

So during that May 4th Movement which Sun was intervening in, to build into a republican movement, he polemicized against what he saw as the influence of a British irrationalism. He said: "A group intoxicated with a new culture have begun to reject the old morality, saying that the former makes the latter unnecessary. . . . [They say] there are no princes in a de-

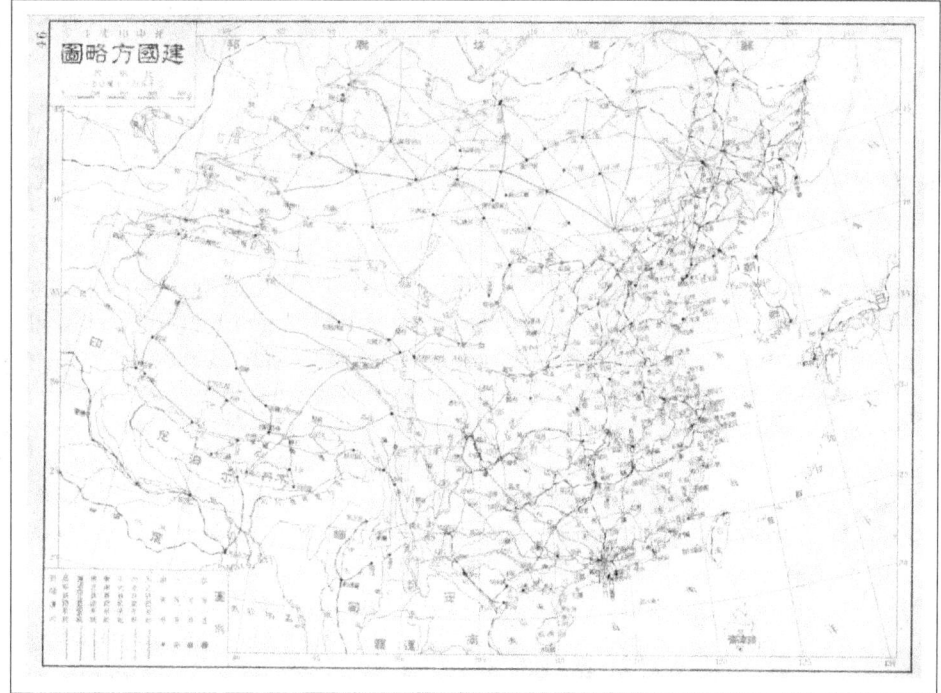

Sun Yat-sen's map for the development of rail and canals for China, 1919. A comparison with China's current extensive rail development shows that Sun's program has finally been realized.

Bertrand Russell

John Dewey

mocracy, so loyalty is not needed and can be cast away."

He identified this ideology with John Stuart Mill, another of the British ideologues, and he said, it would make the 400 million Chinese "like a sheet of loose sand," basically manipulable and not unified.

In 1919, he wrote *The International Development of China,* and you saw these maps yesterday by Prof. Nie Lei, of China's rail developments today: There it is. This is what Sun Yat-sen laid out for the rail and water development of China in 1919, as an international project. So in fact, what Xi Jinping and the Chinese are doing today, is literally realizing that movement.

The British recognized the extreme danger of Sun Yat-sen's American System intervention into China, and had to *crush* it. So they sent one of their top, top agents, Bertrand Russell, whom Lyndon LaRouche has declared the most evil man in the 20th Century. He was sponsored by the Anti-Religious Society. He argued that Christianity was the bane of the West, and that Confucianism was the cause of backwardness in China. He wrote a book called *The Problem of China,* which is entirely a "noble savage" piece, saying that we should leave them happy in the mud, basically as Daoists, happy as farmers with no science, no technology.

This is his quote: "Chinese officials are, as a rule, corrupt and indolent, so that control by foreigners is necessary in creating a modern bureaucracy, and to prepare the way for the creation of an efficient Chinese state.

"Instinctive happiness, or joy of life, is one of the most important goods that we have lost through industrialism.... Progress and efficiency, for example, make

no appeal to the Chinese, except to those who have come under western influence. By valuing progress and efficiency, we have secured power and wealth; by ignoring them, the Chinese, until we brought disturbance, secured on the whole a peaceable existence and a life full of enjoyment."

John Dewey

The noble savage: Keep the people backward and we can continue our control. Russell was a libertine and a homosexual; what he most despised in Confucianism, was the honoring of the family. He said that honoring the family was holding the country back. He said that in China, the Malthus theory of overpopulation "finds full scope." There are too many people. One thing Dr. Wang didn't get to—but it's in his writings—is that Benjamin Franklin aspired to have America be as populous as China. That's what he wanted.

And John Dewey—I won't go through it now—he came to China from the United States, but he was working for JP Morgan, who was running the British takeover of the American banking system. He was the deschooler. He said you should learn by doing; you shouldn't learn from textbooks. You should all go out and dig in the dirt. I bring this up because Russell and Dewey—the words, "Russell and Dewey," are very, very well known in China. People know that these were the people who brought "Western" thinking to China during the May 4th Movement.

And really, what happened was that 45 years later, their ideas were implemented in China in the Cultural Revolution. Schools were shut down, people were sent out to work with the farmers, scientists were attacked and killed—it was a nightmare for China, and it was these ideas, these British ideas, which gave birth to it—there's a lot more to say about that, but they basically gave birth to what became that nightmare.

One last thing is this fellow, Joseph Needham. I'm sure none of you, except the Chinese here, have heard of Joseph Needham. The Chinese know him very well. He was one of the great British lovers of China! He loved China. He wrote seventeen volumes of *Science and Civilization in China.* He's praised as somebody who "respected" the fact that the Chinese had developed great scientific ideas. And some of what he documents is true.

But what's his purpose? His purpose was to show that all the great scientific developments in China—Let's look at it this way: He had something called the "Needham question," which was discussed among all China scholars for a long, long time. This was: "Why did the development of China stop, when the Renaissance took place in the West?" What made it stop? Was his answer, the Venetian Empire, the Venetian empiricists who shut down the collaboration? Was it the British Opium Wars?

No. It was Confucianism. That's what stopped China's progress. And to explain how they had great science, he said it was mysticism that gave rise to science. Magic gives rise to science, not Confucianism.

Here's Joseph Needham's quote: "Rationalism proved itself less favorable than mysticism to the progress of science. ... Science and magic are in their earlier stages indistinguishable." I'm not kidding.

"Rational theology was anti-scientific; mystical theology proved to be pro-scientific. ... Thus, the interest taken in the early Royal Society in what we now can see were magical claims."

Indeed, you probably know about when Newton's case was opened up, after they had initially refused to allow anybody to open his trunk. When they opened it, it turned out that Newton was a raving mystical fanatic, a believer in magic. Which explains why Leibniz was able to basically show that Newton was a fraud as a scientist.

So, Needham also had to explain, somehow, how the great period of scientific development in China came during that Song Dynasty Renaissance, which was the Confucian Renaissance under Zhu

Joseph Needham

Xi. Well, it was pretty simple for Needham: He just basically said that Zhu Xi called himself a Confucian but he was really a Daoist. And Leibniz—who loved Zhu Xi—was a Daoist, too. I won't go into the details, we don't have time. But it's a fascinating story.

I think I can close with that. We now have this Confucian Renaissance: the Confucian Institutes around the world. I think there's a problem, still, in China. Joseph Needham is still thought of as a great hero by the Chinese.

Oh, by the way, on Joseph Needham: During the Cultural Revolution, he went to China, and then he wrote and he spoke all over the world saying that this is the greatest revolution in Chinese history. Going back to the stone age! And there's more to say about Needham.

But the traditions of Russell and Dewey, the traditions of Yen Fu, and the traditions of Needham are still very strong in China. This is what Xi Jinping is working against. This is what he had to root out, and still has to root out. These are fundamental issues, which are being fought out there, and luckily, in China, the humanists are winning. We have to link up with that tradition in China, just as we have to link up with our best traditions in the West, in order to realize the kind of Renaissance which we have to bring about. And to do that, the evil of the British system, indeed, must be crushed. We have to. We won't survive if we don't.

So we need to know that the tremendously inspiring presentation that Helga gave this morning, was the basis on which we can move ourselves to the mission that we do have as a human race, but we do have to recognize that we have to crush this British system if we're going to make it work.

Thank you.

MEMORANDUM

LaRouche on the Subject of B.G. Tilak's Thesis:[1]

The Present Scientific Implications of Vedic Calendars from the Standpoint of Kepler and Circles of Gauss

by Lyndon H, LaRouche, Jr.

FUSION ENERGY FOUNDATION

Jan 29, 1984

Work reviewing the historical implications of early Vedic astronomical calendars, by FEF and some among its collaborators, is an included feature of several years ongoing work by an international team co-directed by FEF co-director Dr. Uwe V. Parpart and Lyndon H. La-Rouche, Jr., chief executive for an international news-weekly, the **Executive Intelligence Review**.[2]

This research-project was actually begun as a collaboration between Parpart and LaRouche beginning the early 1970s, and was continued as an integral part of the historical researches into the roots of modem science by the staff of FEF. This program has emphasized attention to primary published and unpublished documents, with emphasis on previously unknown as well as generally neglected materials available only in documentary deposits of specialist archives in various parts of the world.

The central objective of this particular work has been to uncover and correlate evidence from a wide range of primary sources bearing upon the principles and methods of scientific discovery employed at various points in the emergence of mathematical physics and related subject-matters. The practical objective of this specialized work is the development of new elements to be supplied to improved educational curricula, elements selected for the purpose of fostering an increase in the students' potentials for scientific discovery.

We have been able to show how the work of Nicholas of Cusa and other leading figures of the fifteenth-century Golden Renaissance set into motion the extraordinary, skyrocketing development of modern mathematical physics. Cusa's **Docta Ignorantia** is most exemplary of writings with a powerful influence on the scientific work of Leonardo da Vinci and successors such as Kepler, Gilbert, Desargues, Leibniz, et al., either directly or indirectly. Cusa's work was chiefly addressed to classical-Greek sources, including the work of Archimedes most emphatically. This view of the classical Greeks from the standpoint of the Golden Renaissance implies the question: Whence did those Greeks, in turn, acquire their inspiration?

About 1981, largely on the initiative of Dr. Parpart, we focused on the work of leading centers of Sanskrit studies in India, centers which have been developed on the foundations of the German school of classical philology of Humboldt, Bopp, and Boeckh. In this connection, our attention was drawn to two of the books of the Indian patriot-scholar Bal Gangadhar Tilak, Tilak's **Orion** [1893] and **Arctic Home in the Vedas** [1903]. Employing studies of ancient Vedic astronomical calendars conducted chiefly by German astronomers and physicists, including the circles of Karl Gauss, Tilak dated the earliest versions of some Vedic hymns to not later than 4,000 B.C., when the relevant equinox was in the constellation of Orion. In the **Arctic Home**, Tilak extended what he had begun in **Orion**, exploring the implications of astonishingly accurate polar long-cycles and related matter in transmitted epic poetry of the Indo-European literature. The question was posed:

---

1. Lyndon H. LaRouche, Jr. is a member of the board of directors of the Fusion Energy Foundation.
2. The **Executive Intelligence Review**'s annual subscription price ($396 in the U.S.A.) properly implies its specialist quality, serving the economic policy and related needs of executives worldwide.

Bal Gangadhar Tilak

Could such provably pre-Mesopotamian datings for a rigorous early astronomy supply important parts of the answer to our questions respecting the early roots of scientific thinking?

In aid of this quest, we focused attention on several areas bearing upon these questions, including review of the work of German astronomers who had studied the Vedic long-cycle astronomical calendars. In general, we brought to bear our earlier work on classical Greek philosophy and philology, examining the Vedic materials of relevance from this standpoint of reference.

Although the amount of usable material from Sanskrit sources is, understandably, if frustratingly meager in amount, there is enough which is both incontestable and crucial, that re-examining the development of European scientific methods and thought in the setting of Vedic evidence proved most fruitful in several ways.

The purpose of this present report is to provoke discussion of the project summarized among a broader circle of specialists, in addition to informing FEF mem-

bers of this aspect of our ongoing research-activities. We believe strongly that there are lessons to be adduced by aid of such studies which will be useful stimulants to some engaged in fundamental research in physics-laboratories today.

First, we outline the points of departure we have employed for correlating this and related information.

The LaRouche-Riemann Method

The bench-mark for this and other undertakings has been the exceptionally successful methods employed in the **Executive intelligence Review**'s quarterly forecasts for the U.S. economy, published regularly beginning November 1979.[3] This is the outgrowth of a discovery made by LaRouche during 1952, that the methods of Bernard Riemann (1820-1866) permitted implicit measurement of the causal connection between introduction of improved technologies and resulting increases in potential rates of economic growth, on condition that the definition and measurement of technology follows the pioneering definitions of technology supplied by Gottfried Leibniz.

Leibniz's development of the foundations of economic science is fairly summarized as follows.

Leibniz's development of economic science, as distinct from pre-existing doctrines of *cameralism*, centered around exploration of the principles of the heat-powered machine; most emphatically the relationship between the consumption of an amount of coal to power a machine, and the resulting increase in the output of an operative obtained by employment of such a heat-powered machine. In the hypothetical case, that two machines consume the same amounts of coal per hour, but that the same operative obtains greater output from the use of the one than the other, the difference in performance is attributable to the internal organization of the machine. This difference in organization defines the notion of *technology*, or, in eighteenth-century French usages, such as the Monge-Carnot Ecole Polytechnique modeled upon Leibniz's influence, *polytechnique*.

In the simplest cases, the organization of a powered machine may be studied in terms of normalized circular action. The changes in direction of application of trans-

---

3. This quarterly forecast is called the "LaRouche-Riemann" forecast because its computer-assisted application employs Riemann's 1859 "On The Propagation of Plane Air Waves of Finite Magnitude" as the model for precalculating phase-changes within economies.

mitted power, plus changes in the energy-flux density of the power applied, are central points of consideration. Leibniz treats this approach as subsumed by his notion of a Principle of Least Action.

In the more generalized case, in the complex domain, self-similar conical-spiral action supersedes circular action. The conical form of self-similar spiral action is the normal elementary representation of *work*, and the cylindrical form of self-similar spiral action represents the transmitting of *energy* without work accomplished. By normalizing statements about technology according to these terms of reference, technology is implicitly measurable, and that measurement correlates with potential of increased rates of economic growth for the case of a properly normalized description of an economic process.

In Leibniz's first approximation, the notion of *work* was derived from simple comparison of rates of output of defined products by an operative: the object of the heat-powered machine was defined by reference to increasing an operative's power to produce an increased number of useful objects of a specific quality.

In the LaRouche-Riemann method, the implicit fallacies of such an assumption are emphasized. *How do we determine the relative usefulness of an object produced? How do we determine whether to increase the output of product "A," rather than devoting that allocable effort to production of more of "B" and "C"?* The customary approaches to interpreting the "allocation problem" are avoided by the LaRouche-Riemann method.

Instead, the *increase of the potential relative population-density* of a society is employed as the standard of measure of *work* accomplished within that society, and particular production is treated as an implicit contribution to increase of the potential relative population-density for the society as a whole.

The importance of this choice of measurement of *work* is shown most directly by reference to the hypo-

Gottfried Wilhelm Leibniz (1646-1716).

thetical case in which a society abruptly halts technological progress. Continued reinvestment of profits and "replacement funds" combined, under conditions of fixed technology, is inherently entropic. Since neither living processes nor societies can endure for long unless they are characteristically negentropic, the preconditions for indefinite existence of a society/economy is technological progress. Those activities within society which implicitly increase the potential relative population-density must represent, therefore, either the introduction or mediation of advances in technology. It is the aspect of production (etc.) which initiates/mediates advances in technology which contributes work.

So, the indicated correlation of technology and economic growth is feasible and required.

This requires that we attempt to correlate the kinds of mental activity of individuals which generate or mediate advances in technology with implicitly measurable technology. We must define topological congruence between creative-mental processes, so defined, and those transformations in functions of a continuous manifold which correspond to advances in technology. To accomplish this, we must shift attention away from particular inventions to *species* of invention; we must correlate a *species* of creative mental transformation in mental behavior with a correlated *species* of advances in generalized forms of technology.[4]

We organize the study of the mental processes of creative discovery according to Plato's notion of a hypothesis of the higher hypothesis. We follow Plato also in requiring that all statements developed bearing upon the subject of hypothesis must be stated as principles of geometry. However, the form of geometry which meets this requirement is of the form of a synthetic geometry.

---

4. Criton Zoakos has pointed out the fallacy of translating the Greek into "idea" or "form" in connection with Plato's work; the best English equivalent would be "species."

In such a synthetic geometry, no axioms, postulates, or deductive methods are permitted. In the case of a geometry of visible space, only circular action, as defined by the isoperimetric principle, is "self evident"; all other forms must be derived by a "hereditary" principle of construction from circular action so defined. In higher geometry, the geometry of a continuous manifold, the self-similar conical form of spiral action, the elementary complex variable, takes the place occupied by circular action in the discrete manifold of visible space.

The notion of a hypothesis of the higher hypothesis is defined by considering three distinct kinds of hypothesis. This leads directly to a statement subsuming both the nature of creative-mental activity and the congruence of such activity with advances in technology.

Simple Hypothesis. Any prevailing body of ideas about man and the universe, most clearly and simply mathematical science, can be interpreted as a logical latticework defined everywhere by some "hereditary principle." This principle may be either of the syllogistic or constructive species. In the case of a syllogistic lattice-work, all theorems have embedded in them reflections of the axioms and postulates upon which the elaboration of the lattice-work is premised. Similarly, although a synthetic geometry has no such deductive or axiom-postulate features, the point of departure of the geometry, and the principle of construction employed, is an hereditary feature of the geometry as a whole.

In the case that an hypothesis is formulated, and that the formulation is strictly defined by standards of consistency with an existing body of knowledge, the hypothesis so formulated is a *simple hypothesis.*

The practical implications are clearer as we turn our attention to the subject of *higher hypothesis.*

The second class of hypothesis, *higher hypothesis,* violates consistency with existing bodies of thought in a special and rigorous manner. In this instance, we assume that some axiomatic, or kindred feature of existing scientific knowledge (for example) is fallacious or inadequate. To that purpose, we define an experi-

Nicholas of Cusa

mental observation whose specific subject-matter is some crucial evidence which suffices to overthrow the axiomatic or kindred assumption in question.

All fundamental scientific discoveries, for example, are of the form of crucial, sufficient proof of such a higher hypothesis. The socratic method, or what Plato identifies as his *dialectical method,*[5] is based on such critical examinations of generally accepted underlying assumptions. In that respect, socratic method and creative-mental activity are of the same species.

If it is shown that successive scientific revolutions, for example, are an orderable series, then it is so illustrated that successive higher hypotheses are implicitly subsumed by some definable principle of progressive discovery, such that the principle itself remains substantially the same through a series of successive scientific revolutions; that although those revolutions contradict one another in certain key fundamentals, all members of that series are nonetheless consistent with some definable principle of discovery sufficient to account for the generation of the higher hypothesis in each case. Such a principle of discovery is the subject of a special hypothesis, an hypothesis generating a series of higher hypotheses: a *hypothesis of the higher hypothesis.*

This hypothesis of the higher hypothesis is implicitly subject to experimental demonstration and definitions. That is, there are experiments which explore such an hypothesis as the principle subject-matter directly considered. Cusa's **Docta Ignorantia** is exemplary of the approach to be taken. Cusa's work on geometry and scientific method, the work of Luca Pacioli and Leonardo da Vinci, the work of Kepler, Leibniz, Gauss, Riemann, and Cantor, are exemplary of the main currents

---

5. This is not to be confused with the "dialectical method" of either G.W.F. Hegel or Karl Marx. Hegel's **Phenomenology** and other of his relevant writings are "delphic" parodies or Aristotle's treatment of Plato's method, but also directly opposed to Plato on all matters of fundamental principles. The best modern examples of masters of dialectical method are Nicholas of Cusa and the socratic dialogues composed by Gottfried Leibniz.

of continued attention to this subject. The rigorous elaboration of a synthetic geometry, first for the discrete manifold of visible space, and then for the continuous manifold, is the best example of concrete definitions of an hypothesis of the higher hypothesis.

Our own work on this subject was improved significantly by concerted attention to the central thesis of the great Sanskrit philologist Panini. The central feature of the classical philology of Panini[6] is his insistence that all terms of language, and the structure of statements, is derived from the transitive verb. In fact, all rigorous efforts to elaborate philologies and grammars, beginning with Panini's work, are broadly to be divided into two opposing camps: those which, like Panini, derive everything from the transitive verb, and those opposing currents which base grammar on the noun as elementary. The relevance of philology to modern issues of scientific method is illustrated by the point that the scientific method of Cusa, Leonardo, Kepler, Leibniz, Gauss, et al. defines elementary phenomena as of the form of transitive verbs, whereas the empiricists and materialists (e.g., Bacon, Descartes, Newton, et al.) define nouns (names of objects) to be elementary. *These represent two mutually exclusive ways of thinking about man and the universe*, as illustrated by the irreconcilable opposition between platonic *realism* and aristotelean *nominalism*.

In a conception of the universe treating the noun as the elementary unit of thought about sense-experience, the noun is the thing toward which one might point. The result is typified by the Cartesian form of the discrete manifold nouns within empty Euclidean space. This approach leads to axiomatic algebra of the type associated with radical empiricism or neo positivism the simple comparison of magnitudes of countable objects. This also defines the substrate of the syllogism: the syllogism prohibits the statement of action or cause as such within the statement: *action* and *cause* are replaced by the principle of the Middle Term. The notion of hypothetical "instantaneous" existence of objects is also exemplary of the characteristics of a nominalist outlook.

In the opposing, verb-centered philology and philosophical world-outlook, a phenomenon is the smallest possible transformation which is characterized by that transformation as a species.

For example: Luca Pacioli and Leonardo da Vinci were the first known to have reported, that all living processes are distinguished from non-living by a self-similar morphology of development congruent with the Golden Section. Thus, the smallest aspect of a living process which contains this characteristic defines an elementary phenomenon of biology. This does not ignore the chemical composition of organic material; however, chemical composition, and chemical reactions as such, do not define a process as living.

The modern classical case of rejection of the verb-definition of phenomena is Ludwig Boltzmann's doctrine of statistical fluctuations, and the Weiner-Shannon definition of "negentropy" within an "information theory" premised upon the statistical theory of percussive heat. Boltzmann's and related approaches start from the LaPlace version of Descartes' discrete manifold: a noun-form. The "theory of statistical fluctuations" is probably to be credited, at least chiefly, to LaPlace. A worldview premised upon such an assumption must imply the arbitrary postulates superimposed upon thermodynamics by Helmholtz et al., the so-called "laws of thermodynamics." As Newton pointed out, the use of a Cartesian manifold for physics presents a view of the universe in which the universe is necessarily winding-down as the mainspring of a mechanical clock, a point underscored by Leibniz later in the Clarke-Leibniz correspondence. Entropy is a doctrine inherent in the adoption of a nominalist form of discrete manifold, such as Descartes'.

Yet, Kepler had already demonstrated that the laws of astronomy were derived uniquely from geometrical constructions hereditarily derived from the Golden Section. Hence, the universe as a whole had the characteristics otherwise associated with living processes. Although Kepler's doctrine was not adequate, it was proven to be fully valid, relative to all alternatives proposed, by the work of Karl Gauss, et al. Gauss showed also that elliptic functions as projected into the domain of the visible manifold are generated by self-similar conical-spiral action in the continuous manifold.[7] The conical form of such self-similar spiral action is the source, within the continuous manifold, of Golden-Section-ratio characteristics of images projected into the discrete manifold. So, self-similar conical-spiral action in the continuous manifold is the proper geometrical definition of the term *negentropy*. The universe as

---

6. Panini probably wrote during the Fifth Century B.C., as indicated by his reference to Buddhism.

7. See Dr. Jonathan Tennenbaum's treatment of Gauss's "arithmetic-geometric mean." FEF, 1983.

Johannes Kepler *Carl Friedrich Gauss* *Bernhard Riemann*

a whole is essentially negentropic, not entropic; the Kepler-Gauss proofs are conclusive to this effect. The introduction of arbitrary postulates, such as the "laws of thermodynamics," after the work of Gauss had been well established, must be classed as a sophomoric sort of error.

The topological principle of Lejeune Dirichlet, which Riemann repeatedly identifies as "Dirichlet's Principle," is the crucial step making possible Riemann's advances premised on the work of Gauss. The 1854 habilitation dissertation[8], one of three papers which Riemann prepared for that occasion, identifies the principled, central feature of that connection, although only in a preliminary fashion. The "unique experimental" method, defined by Riemann in this location, is exemplary of the need to restrict the definition of empirical phenomena to phenomena defined in terms of transitive verbs [transformations].

If this is applied to Plato's work, it becomes clear at once that the methodological standpoint we have summarily described here is the world-outlook guiding Plato in those writings.

To this, one crucial added point must be attached. The application of the principle of synthetic geometry to Panini's thesis requires that verbs themselves be derivable from a single transitive verb. This elementary transitive verb must be congruent with the notion of

_____
8. Riemann, "On The Hypotheses Which Underlie Geometry."

self-evident circular action in a discrete manifold, and self-similar conical-spiral action in a continuous manifold. Roughly, the name for this verb must be "to create" or, "to cause oneself to be elaborated." In Judeo-Christian theology, this is the name for the Creator, or, perhaps better, "The Creating." As a matter of human knowledge, that theology would prescribe that we know such a "Creating" only in its aspect as the *Logos* (e.g., of the Gospel of St. John). Plato defines this Logos as an *unhypothesized principle of the Universe*, and as that which progressive development of the hypothesis of the higher hypothesis seeks to reach. This Logos is identified as an efficient existence (therefore *substantial*), and consubstantial with the "Creating," named in Plato's **Timaeus**, the *Composer*. [The practical significance of identifying the theological connection will be clear once we examine the implications of Tilak's thesis as such.]

Creating and *negentropy* have the same significance, on condition that negentropy is defined geometrically, as we have stipulated above. Those aspects of human mental life which correspond to the hypothesis of the higher hypothesis, and to the revolutionary activity of the higher hypothesis, are the only aspects of our thinking properly, usefully described as creative-mental activity.

Drs. Parpart and Bardwell, and their collaborators, have estimated the potential human population of the Earth to be approximately ten million under conditions of a "hunting and gathering society": in the order of about ten square kilometers is required to sustain an average person. The human population today is rapidly approaching three orders of magnitude beyond that—provided we do not plunge into a New Dark Age during the remaining years of the present century. No animal species could willfully effect an increase of potential relative population-density of even a significant fraction of one order of magnitude. The difference between human and animal species on this account is those creative-mental potentials we associate with the generation and mediation of revolutionary advances in technology. It is these qualities which make us human, as distinct from those inferior aspects of our nature [individual irrationalist hedonism, for example] which we share in common with the beasts.

It may be observed that even in those features of individual behavior which are clearly directed by irrationalistic hedonistic impulses, human behavior is qualitatively "more sophisticated" than that of the beasts; the use of language by a demented fellow, for example. Yet, the power of speech was not developed by the bestial impulse which employs it in that instance; a development of human speech accomplished through the action of creative-mental life, has been, in that instance, appropriated by a base impulse. Human individuals, and societies, are a conflict between the creative-mental potentials of the individual and those baser, irrationalist, hedonist, impulses which partake of the beast. The individual, the society is a product of the interaction of two opposing qualities of generative impulses.

Before turning to the implications of Tilak's thesis, one crucial point must be clarified.

Up to this point, we have treated the hypothesis of the higher hypothesis as if such a principle of discovery were more or less fixed in character, except as we indicated Plato's view of the development of such an hypothesis toward sought agreement with the Logos. That simplified view, employed up to this point, was adopted as a pedagogical device: to emphasize that the character of that hypothesis is such, that if the principle were fixed in quality it would implicitly generate a sequence of successive higher hypotheses.

In reality, the hypothesis of the higher hypothesis develops through the effects of higher hypotheses. The best example of the form of this change, *this perfecting process*, is the emergence of the notion of the complex domain, especially beginning the work to this effect by Karl Gauss. From Plato onward, it was a principle that the visible world is a distorted image of the real universe, like the shadows cast by firelight on the rough walls of a darkened cave. The idea of a transfinite, superior to the visible world, of which the visible world affords us only distorted images, is a common feature of Plato, Cusa, and so on. Yet, the internal features of the real world, the world of the continuous manifold [complex domain] were not solved to the degree that the synthetic geometry of the visible domain was explored.

Although this was not generally accepted even at Göttingen University during the later-nineteenth or early-twentieth centuries, the standpoint running into Riemann, which Riemann represented most clearly and emphatically, is that the transfinite domain [the complex domain of the continuous manifold] is the location of efficient substantiality. On this account, that view is sometimes associated with the name of "ontologically transfinite." Looking from Riemann back through Gauss, Leibniz, Cusa, to Plato, there is no point of principled inconsistency between Riemann's view and that of these predecessors. Yet, the mastery of the internal geometry of the complex domain, begun so clearly by Gauss, represents a decisive breakthrough in richer form of an hypothesis of the higher hypothesis.

More practically, a well-ordered economy is one whose direction of development is supplied by "science driver" institutions, such as the Monge-Carnot Ecole Polytechnique, the Manhattan Project, the NASA research-and-development phase, and so forth. The most effective kind of science-driver institution would be one which arranged its efforts to identify and attack those frontiers of scientific inquiry on which revolutions respecting fundamentals were located. The objective is to achieve something analogous to what Gauss achieved in enriching the hypothesis of the higher hypothesis, to improve the hypothesis of higher hypothesis, as a principle of discovery, to the effect of making it more powerful.

It is this standpoint, pivoted on the LaRouche-Riemann method, which is applied to the case of Tilak's thesis.

'Arctic Home'

Combining Sanskrit philology with European astronomers' work on Vedic long-cycle astronomical calendars, Bal Gangadhar Tilak developed two successive, coherent theses, which he himself combined into a single thesis in his later work, **Arctic Home**. In the first work, **Orion**, Tilak showed that the earliest Vedic hymns, including those containing crucial calendar information, must be dated to earlier than 4,000 B.C., during the period the relevant equinox coincided with the constellation of Orion. In the second, **Arctic Home**, he focused on the fact that the ancient astronomical calendars transmitted through the Vedic referenced north-polar constellations, coinciding with transmission of other references to polar constellations and legends in the Vedic and Zend Avesta.

To provide the flavor of Tilak's own thought on the matter, the following excerpt from the Preface of his 1903 **The Arctic Home** is supplied here:

This present volume is a sequel to my **Orion** or *Researches into the Antiquity of the Vedas*, published in 1893. The estimate of Vedic antiquity then generally current amongst Vedic scholars was based on the assignment of arbitrary period of time to the different strata into which the Vedic literature is divided; and it was believed that the oldest of these strata could not at the best, be older than 2,400 B.C. In my **Orion**, however, I tried to show that all such estimates, besides being too modest, were vague and uncertain, and that the astronomical statements found in the Vedic literature supplied us with far more reliable data for correctly ascertaining the ages of the different periods of Vedic literature. These astronomical statements, it was further shown, unmistakably pointed out that the Vernal equinox was in the constellation of Mriga or Orion (about 4,500 B.C.) during the period of the Vedic hymns, and that it had receded to the constellation of the Krittikâs, or the Pleiades (about 2,500 B.C.) in the days of the Brathmanas. . . . But if the age of the oldest Vedic period was thus carried back to 4,500 B.C., one was still tempted to ask whether we had, in that limit, reached the Ultima Thule of the Aryan antiquity. … the conclusion, that the ancestors of the Vedic Rishis lived in an Arctic Home in inter-Glacial times, was forced upon me by the slowly accumulating mass of Vedic and Ayes-tic literature . . . the beginnings of Aryan civilization must be supposed to date back several thousand years before the oldest Vedic period; and when the commencement of the post-Glacial epoch is brought down to 8,000 B.C., it is not at all surprising if the date of Aryan primitive life is found

to go back to it from 4,500 B.C., the age of the oldest Vedic period. There are many passages in the Rig-Veda which plainly disclose the Polar attributes of the Vedic deities, or the traces of an ancient Arctic calendar. When we put them [such Vedic and Avestic references] side by side with what we know of the Glacial and post-Glacial epoch from the latest geological researches, we can not avoid the conclusions that the primitiveAryan home was both Glacial and inter Glacial."[9]

The principal fact we are emphasizing by aid of reference to Tilak's thesis, is Tilak's reliance on a fact already well-established by German astronomers approximately a century before Tilak's writing: *the first known trace of a rigorous mathematical science, astronomy, antedates all of the cultures of the Mesopotamian and Egyptian-dynastic series by some thousands of years.*

The LaRouche-Riemann method enables us to accomplish two things which could not be undertaken either by astronomy alone, or by application of Sanskrit philology to the astronomical-calendar evidence from the Vedic sources. First, by using the LaRouche-Riemann method, we are able to show that the astronomical-calendar evidence suffices to demonstrate conclusively certain characteristic features of the culture which produced such ancient calendars. Second, from the standpoint of the hypothesis of the higher hypothesis. Situated within the LaRouche-Riemann method, the calendar evidence, added to already explored evidence on the recent 2,500 years development of European science, permits us to offer more general, more fundamental conclusions bearing on the principled features of scientific progress than have been otherwise available.

The initially stunning feature of the ancient calendars is the inclusion of some very long astronomical cycles, including such cycles for the North geologic and *magnetic* Poles. Most stunning of all, the determination of the cycle for the movement of the magnetic North Pole could be accomplished by an ancient culture only were that culture *a well-developed maritime culture.*

The LaRouche-Riemann method corroborates such evidence's implications, by showing that the conditions

9. 1958 reprint, Poona, India, 196, pp. i-vi.

of "hunting-and-gathering culture" are such, that the transition from a primitive food-gathering culture to a civilized series of cultures can be accomplished in only one general way, through only one aspect of the spectrum of primitive food-gathering activities. That aspect of food-gathering activities is fishing, especially near the mouths of large river-systems.

This is readily shown, by restating population-density in the language of thermodynamics. Of all the potential energy available in an average square-kilometer of habitable area, human practice at any level of development is able to obtain only a fraction of that total as usable energy employed to sustain human existence. In the food-gathering culture, this is expressible by such statements as that approximately ten square-kilometers are required to sustain an average individual.[10]

The case of fishing near mouths of large river systems is an exception to this general picture. The development of such fishing along coastal regions is the precondition for emergence of urban-like settlements. The usable energy available per square-kilometer of food-gathering activity, is the critical parameter in this case. The development of a maritime culture, associated with urban sites, is demonstrably the precondition for the production of the "agricultural revolution."

Our best archeological information known to be available today dates the "agricultural revolution" to not later than approximately 8,000 B.C. This is based on traces of seed-varieties demonstrably products of a process of cultivation. In European legends, that evidence coincides with the overlay of Plato's report on Egyptian accounts of the fall of an Atlantis culture [circa 10,000 B.C.] and the account of the Atlas people in Didorus Siculus. As we shall note, in due course, here, there are internal features of the account in Didorus Siculus which oblige us to regard it as largely history, rather than myth. According to the Atlas people, their ancestors were taught agriculture by a colonizing maritime culture. It is certainly the case, that the optimal circumstance for development of an agricultural revolution is a wide-ranging maritime culture's impact upon innovations in plant cultivation near the urban sites of such a culture.

The Atlas account also indicates the people who arrived in boats, to establish an urban colony in the vicinity of the Straits of Gibraltar, introduced an astronomical calendar, a point indicated by the "sky god" in what the Atlas people jovially assured Didorus Siculus was no religious pantheon, but a mythologized version of leading figures of the colony in that vicinity. A maritime culture requires astronomy of some degree, and urban sites are a precondition for development of an astronomy attributed to the pre-Vedic definitions of long cycles.

It is rather obvious that the use of stone structures for astronomical observations, and the observation of constellations in conjunction with measurement of the sidereal year, the solar year, and progression of the equinox, constitute the rudiments of an early form of rigorous astronomy. The addition of a lodestone at such observatories, and the use of such a version of Ulysses' "spirit of the ship" for maritime navigation, constitutes an adequate repertoire for producing an astronomy of the type indicated for Vedic and pre-Vedic calendars. These constitute the clearly adducible characteristics of Vedic and pre-Vedic astronomy.

On the matter of ancient trans-Atlantic, and trans-Pacific maritime cultures, the arguments mustered in opposition to such propositions are clearly arbitrary nonsense. Admittedly, the fact that one argument is nonsensical does not show that every variety of counter argument is therefore valid; the fact that it is absurd arbitrariness to argue against the existence of trans-Atlantic maritime culture does not show that every mythical or imagined account of such trans-Atlantic cultures is therefore valid. [Otherwise, a statistician might argue, as some have said, that since there must be either life on Mars or not, the probability of life on Mars is 50%.] Exemplary of the nonsense is the public display of laborious efforts to locate the travels of the Odyssey entirely within the Mediterranean. "Homer's" text describes with striking precision, a journey through the Straits of Gibraltar, across into the Caribbean, back to northern Europe and down to Greece. This would have required a long-boat [much resembling a later Viking long-boat] of the sort which proliferated during no later than the second millennium B.C. among "Peoples of the Sea," and would have been greatly advantaged by a compass—the "spirit of the ship." Certainly, the pre 1,000 B.C. cultures in Yucatan were far more advanced than later Mayan habitations of the same region, and also, contrary to myth, the Genoese Columbus was guided in his famous travels by aid of a map provided him: the trans-Atlantic traffic has been provably con-

10. At an average life-expectancy significantly lower than twenty years, in circumstances more precarious than the faster, stronger baboon's.

The Sea Peoples in their ships during the battle with the Egyptians. Relief from the mortuary temple of Ramesses III at Medinet Habu.

siderable over the millennia, apart from the not inconsiderable point that the evidence, although chiefly conclusive, is sparse and fragmentary.

More troublesome is the matter of the Arctic Home for such a maritime culture during either the inter-Glacial or immediate post-Glacial period. That this must have occurred prior to 8,000 B.C. is clear enough. What is troublesome is the question whether this began during the approximately 10,000 years of glacial melt preceding 8,000 B.C., or during the glacial period itself.

We have in currency two sets of general accounts of the last Ice Age. One account has the glaciation radiating into the North American and Eurasian continents from the polar ice. This account is by no means conclusively demonstrated. The second account associates the Ice Age with entry of the Gulf Stream into the polar region, melting the ice-cap, and contributing to the deposit of glaciation upon the adjoining continents.

Unless we associate the pre-Vedic polar culture in question with special cases like the Alaskan land-bridge, the astronomical-calendar evidence requires the Gulf Stream version of the Ice Age, and points to a stunning antiquity for that culture.

Only a few features of this discussion of the antiquity of the early astronomical calendars are essential correlatives of Tilak's **Arctic Home** thesis. However, we must not overlook the fact that some Soviet specialist has proposed diverting the Gulf Steam into the Arctic, an endeavor which might be suicidal for the Soviet Union, as well as destructive of much of Europe and North America. What is essential, and also demonstrated, is that we must locate an ancient maritime culture significantly prior to 8,000 B.C., and as existing within the polar region.

It is noteworthy that only a maritime-fishing culture would have lived in a quasi-temperate Arctic region [when ocean-levels were as much as hundreds of feet lower than today] during the long Arctic night. Since early astronomical calendars were produced there, those calendars must have been produced under such cultural conditions.

It is also strongly indicated, that the "riparian model" of development of civilization is defective to the point of being a fallacy of composition of evidence, and in key respects a deliberate falsification of the overwhelming evidence to the contrary by those who have been influenced by the same "theory of stages" of human development made famous [or, notorious] by Adam Smith, first, and then Hegel and the Marxists, such as Karl Wittvogel, V. Gordon Childe, et al. There was "riparian" development, of course: water and energy are the essence of agricultural production. This riparian development was an offshoot of broad development of maritime culture. The leading points of absurdity of conjectural portraits such as that of the Marxist V. Gordon Childe, are now to be examined, providing the bridge-discussion leading into summary of the second of the two points to be developed here.

The 'Whore of Babylon'

In the modern social sciences, including archeology, all general social theories rampant today are based directly or indirectly upon the arbitrary assumption, that civilized history begins with the Mesopotamian culture of Sumer. General social theory imposes the cultural model concocted for the Mesopotamian series of cultures beginning with the Chaldeans, and interprets everything from psychology to general theory of mathematics-history in a way consistent with the Chaldean mythology.

Most interesting, on this point, is the rather hysterical insistence among archeologists generally, that although some contact between the Sumerian and Harrapan culture [of India] must be conceded, the two cultures must be treated as distinct. The evidence is overwhelming to the contrary. First, the Harrapan culture was vastly more extensive, and more advanced technologically than the Sumerian and Chaldean. Moreover, the Sumerians' insistence that they were a "black-headed people," so distinguished from their semitic neighbors, implies that they were Dravidians. The statement, by Herodotus, that the philistines originated in India, makes sense if interpreted from this standpoint: the philistine's theology, like the Chaldeans from which philistine culture emerged, was Harrapan.

The Harrapan pantheon was dominated by a mother-earth goddess, *Shakti*, and her phallus-symbol consort, *Siva*. This Shakti is the same goddess as the Chaldean *Ishtar*, identified by the New Testament as the "Whore of Babylon." She is the Egyptian *Isis*, the Sabean *Athtar*, the Philistine's *Astarte-Venus* [whence Phoenicia, Venice], the phrygian *Cybele*, and the Russian *Matushka Rus*. Siva is also the Egyptian *Osiris*, the semitic *Satan*, and the consort of Cybele, *Dionysos*. Similarly, the Egyptian *Horus* is the philistine "St. George" cult's figure—imported from the orient, by way of Venice and Genoa, into thirteenth-century England. Horus is also *Lucifer*, and *Apollo*.

The point is not "merely" that these indicated religions were one and the same, at least as differing sects of the same religion may be the same on common essentials. Religion is the most efficient element of the cultural determination of both conscious and unconscious mental behavior, and hence the social practice shaped by human judgment. Any religion can be mapped as a latticework characterized by "hereditary features," features which expressed the embedding of certain axiomatic elements of belief in each and every "theorem" consistent with that religious belief as a whole. These axioms of religious beliefs are chiefly four:

1. The ontological nature of God;
2. The ordering of universal creation;
3. The existence of individual man within universal creation;
4. The relationship between God and individual man with respect to the elaboration of universal creation.

If one knows what actual or implicit religious beliefs are embedded in the prevailing aspects of a culture, one can predict broadly the behavioral characteristics of that culture over spans of generations. The four indicated axiomatic features of belief are key to such determinations.

All of the characteristic features of cultures and cultural-political factions associated with the "Whore of Babylon's" religious-belief matrix are consistent with the indications supplied by examining the Whore of Babylon from the four-fold standpoint indicated. In that sense, the Harrapan and Mesopotamian cultures are identical. This applies also to the Isis-Osiris-Horus cults of Egypt, of the Roman imperial "mystery religions" (Gnosis), and the Gnostic and Sufi cults spawned with aid of Byzantine emperors of the first millennium A.D., beginning with Constantine. The Assyrian, Babylonian, Persian, and other "empires" of the Mesopotamian series, and the Roman, Byzantine, Ottoman, Austro-Hungarian, and Russian empires later, are each and all forms of social organization, of political institutions, of law, and so forth, consistent with the religious-cultural matrix of the Shakti-Whore of Babylon species.

These Whore-of-Babylon cultural species are of an opposite character, directly opposite cultural matrix, not only to the Judaism of Moses and Philo of Alexandria, as well as the Christianity of St. Augustine and the Apostles. On this point, Judeo-Christian belief and culture are ecumenically congruent with the classical-Greek republican culture as typified by Solon of Athens, the tragedies of Aeschylos, the geometrical principles of design of the Acropolis, and the dialogues of Plato. There are echoes of this platonic-neoplatonic cultural matrix in crucial features of the Vedic and pre-Vedic astronomical calendars; that, as we shall identify and summarize the argument a space ahead, here, is key to the second point under consideration.

Friedrich Schiller, who was a leading historian of his time,[11] as well as poet-dramatist and leading thinker of the German republican circles of his last decade of life, proposed that 2,500 years of Mediterranean-European history be ordered by analysis as pivoting upon a conflict between two opposing forces: the republican current traceable to Solon of Athens, and the oligarchical current typified by the Sparta of the mythical Lycurgus, Sparta and Greek [Cadmian] Thebes are cultures modeled upon the Whore-of-Babylon religious-cultural matrix. The republican current of classical Greece, and Apostolic Christianity, define the same general cultural current and converge upon kindred forms of political institutions and social practices. The way in which such opposing religious-cultural matrices bear upon matters of scientific method is adduced most easily by considering three distinct types of professed monotheisms in

---

11. Schiller was Professsor of Universal History at the University of Jena.

terms of the four axiomatic features indicated above. All professed monotheisms are broadly divided between nominally rationalist and professedly irrationalist theologies. Irrationalist monotheisms and polytheisms are essentially interchangeable in axiomatic features; our treatment of irrationalist monotheism thus subsumes the crucial features of the polytheisms. Of the rationalist theologies, these include two mutually-exclusive species. Hence, it is sufficient to consider only three categories of theologies to encompass all the principal forms of culture to be considered.

Nominally rationalist theologies are divided into two species. In the first, the elementary phenomena of religious-cultural belief are of the form of transitive verbs. In the opposing, second species, the terms of elementary notions are in the form of nouns. This distinction was emphasized by Panini, for example. By rigorous implication, the elementary mathematical-ontological thinking of the former species of culture is geometric, as we have summarily specified synthetic geometry. The second species, based on the noun-form, takes the standpoint of arithmetic. treating the ordinal-cardinal integers as the only axiomatic reality of mathematics.[12]

So, we have the four axiomatic features of each of the three species, as follows.

Rational-Geometric

1. God as the "Creating," a consubstantiality of the efficient, substantial principle of creating of the universe [i.e., Logos] consubstantial with the unity of the transfinite being [God], who is "I am that I self-elaborate Myself to become."

2. Ordering of Creation. A negentropic universe, such that the Logos is of the form of a negentropic principle of action, a principle congruent with the verb "to live."

3. Individual Man: To the degree man partakes of the irrationalist hedonism of beasts, every individual is born in an infantile condition of "original sin." However, man's creative-mental potential is to bring his will for practice into agreement with the Logos. In this second aspect of man's twofold nature, man is, in the words of Cusa, "in the image of the living God."

4. God and Man: By perfecting his individual will toward agreement with the Logos, man's practice "participates in the work of God" in altering the universe.

---

12. E.g., Leopold Kronecker, Bertrand Russell, et. al.

Rational-Noun

1. God: "God" is defined as a noun, an object. He is the "monarch" of the universe, in the sense of an absolute autocrat.

2. Ordering of Creation: The universe is ordered by unchangeable mechanical laws, of the form of a consistent latticework premised upon Euclidean-like axioms and postulates.

3. Individual Man: Man is a biological object, connected to God by means of a spirit superimposed upon that biological entity.

4. God and Man: Man's duty is to earn merit with God by obeying the monarch-like Will of God.

Irrational-Noun

1. God: God is an absolute monarch of the universe.

2. Ordering of the Universe: God acts as He chooses; only his Will is efficient.[13]

3. Individual Man: Man is a beast with no function but to acquire merit by obedience to the capricious Will of God.

4. God and Man: From moment to moment, God predestines whom shall be made happy and whom destroyed.

Of the latter two [rational-noun, irrational-noun], Nietzsche echoes tradition in classing the first of the two as "Apollonian," and the second as "Dionysian." Sufism is most exemplary of modern forms of Dionysian (e.g., Satanic, Osiris) cults.

In the case of European culture, although the Augustinian matrix distinguishes Christendom from Byzantium, Byzantine Gnosticism and Sufism penetrated the West through the Crusader and other religious monastic orders, and through the oligarchical factions in the West centered upon the old imperial patrician families of Rome and the Guelph/Black Guelph rentier-financier oligarchies centered upon Venice and Genoa. Hence, both the churches and political institutions of Western Europe and the Americas are penetrated by Gnosticism and Sufi irrationalism to greater or lesser degrees, although the Augustinian matrix remains the embattled substrate of Christendom to the present date.

One of the more significant modern conduits for bringing Sufism into Christendom has been the Jesuit order, created to serve as the international secret-intelligence arm of the Venice-centered Black Guelph fac-

---

13. E.g., Bernard of Clairvaux against Abelard of Paris, and also William of Ockham.

René Descartes

Isaac Newton

against the fact that Gottfried Leibniz was first to develop a differential calculus, a first version of which he submitted to a Paris printer in 1676. The specifications for such a calculus were provided by Kepler. Leibniz employed [chiefly] B. Pascal's work on difference-series to solve the task as given by Kepler. Although a chest of Newton's laboratory papers survives, there is no evidence of any papers dedicated to the calculus's development; in fact, the work credited to Newton appears to have been done by Hooke. Dr. Parpart has worked through relevant features of the Leibniz archive, including portions of the 100,000 manuscript papers thus far more or less 80% untouched by scholars, showing that Leibniz's work of the 1673-1676 period on the differential calculus was already far more advanced than anything seen publicly until much later. Some of this is frankly admitted by Charles Babbage's group in the famous paper "Dotage and D-ism."

More significant than the fact of Leibniz's clear priority—by more than a decade—is the difference in character between the two versions of the calculus. Newton's theory of fluxions is a treatment of a then-long-established work on infinite series, directed to objectives which are frankly cabalistic.[151] The system never worked, such that even the British signed, and adopted a delphic version of not only Leibniz's notion, but Leibniz's calculus as such. [Cauchy's doctrine of limits was employed to effect the distorting parody adopted for this purpose.] Leibniz's method was purely geometrical, following Pascal's efforts to determine number-difference series as geometrically determined. Leibniz's analysis situs was an outgrowth of the same method, as was Euler's continuation of this in his work on topology, and the later work of Monge, Gauss, et al., in the same vein.

The Leibniz-Descartes [hence, also Leibniz-Newton differences] are usefully viewed, especially in our present setting, as reflections of the axiomatic differ-

tion. This was recognized early in the history of the Jesuits; Ignatius Loyola narrowly escaped the judgment of the Inquisition on the basis of the naked similarities of his Spiritual Exercises to the Sufi's spiritual discipline. This bears directly on the seventeenth-century eruption of a Jesuit-led campaign against the influence of Cusa, Leonardo, Kepler, et al., through the Genoese-controlled Francis Bacon [against William Gilbert], the Jesuit Robert Fludd against Kepler,[14] and the work of the Jesuit René Descartes. The case of Augustin Cauchy, during the French Restoration period under the Holy Alliance, is analogous to Descartes' case; Cauchy was dispatched to the work of attempting to destroy French science under guidance of Abbot Moigno, whose writings on this matter of policy are luridly explicit. This is key to the Newton-Leibniz controversy, and also to the more important controversy of Leibniz's attack on the threat to science and morals posed by the doctrines of Descartes. The Leibniz-Newton controversy is a central feature of the seventeenth and eighteenth centuries' controversy over method in science.

It is necessary, for clarity here, to summarize a few facts concerning the "differential calculus" controversy. There is no possible argument of competence

---

14. Fludd, whose program has been coopted by the Jungians [such as Wolfgang Pauli], was the Rosicrucean Jesuit Sufi leader who became the grey eminence of the Stuarts during their exile on the continent. He was the architect of what became the London Royal Society (under William Petty) and the establishment of Scottish-Rite "speculative" freemasonry.

15. Newton's papers show him a fanatical cabalist, an adherence rampant among Petty's circles at that time.

ences in philosophical world-outlook typified by the contrast between rational-verb and rational-noun varieties of religious-cultural belief. Descartes' reputation as a geometer is deceptive. If Descartes is seen as the opponent of Cusa, Kepler, Desargues, Fermat, and Pascal, an opponent operating to parody and so refute their extant work, the proper estimate of Descartes' treatment of geometry is more easily reached. At the time Descartes wrote, the work of Cusa, Kepler, et al., was hegemonic among scientific circles, and the work of Desargues, Fermat, and Pascal shaped the immediate environment to which Descartes addressed his attacks upon those predecessors. Descartes was of the rational-noun species, to the effect that his geometry is subsumed by notions which are axiomatically arithmetic. The same is characteristic of Newton's work, and of the underlying issues between Leibniz and Newton's supporters during the eighteenth century [and later].

The nominalist empiricism of Descartes and the London Royal Society served as the historical basis of reference for the development of eighteenth-century "French classical materialism." In this instance, examining the correspondence of Voltaire is most fruitful. The entirety of the operation centered around variously the French Encyclopedia and Robespierre's Jacobins was steered chiefly by the Jesuit order in France, with close collaboration with the heirs of Petty in Britain and the Swiss families of Geneva and Lausanne who sponsored Voltaire, Rousseau, Robespierre, the Duke of Orleans, and Jacques Necker's political positions in France. These were the same circles behind the Physiocrats [Dr. F. Quesnay, et al.], who were in turn purely a Jesuit undertaking. Such antics led to the papal banning of the Jesuits [to Russia] during the last quarter of that century. Thus was established the "French materialist" faction in Russia, opposing Leibniz's Petrograd Academy, the materialist influence which played a key role in shaping the Russian social-democrats and Bolsheviks later. This was, of course, also the basis for the doctrines of Karl Marx himself.

Insofar as the researches of an international team, over more than a decade, have been able to determine, not a single valid scientific discovery bearing on fundamentals of mathematical physics was produced by members of the Descartes-Newton-Cauchy-Maxwell-et al. faction. Some secondary, sometimes useful experimental discoveries, yes, but nothing bearing on fundamentals. Simple hypothesis? Yes. Higher hypothesis? No.

This is characteristic of the Mesopotamian series of cultures, and the empires modeled upon the Chaldean-Babylonian-Persian model: Rome, etc. In each case some major invention is attributed to such a culture, investigation shows that not only did such an invention exist elsewhere earlier, but that the oligarchical culture in question acquired the invention directly from another culture. Looting and plagiarism are not properly classed as particularly original even in the animal kingdom, and are not to be confused with discovery. At best, such cultures have often shown themselves—at least for a period—capable of extending the range of application of scientific principles acquired, but not as capable of generating a genuine scientific-technological revolution.

Had such oligarchical cultures prevailed, mankind would still be in a primitive gathering-stage of economic existence.

Pre-Vedic Astronomy and Philology

Comparing the Mesopotamia series of cultures with the evidence of earlier, pre-Vedic and Vedic astronomical calendars, we must be inclined to the working-assumption that civilization was set into motion by an earlier culture, an earlier culture of religious-cultural characteristics opposite to those of Whore-of-Babylon cultures. As Plato reports, as a matter to which he gives great practical importance in statecraft generally, the rise of civilization during the period from approximately the Eighth through Fourth Centuries B.C. was not merely a revival from the immediately preceding descent of the Mediterranean into a dark age, after the period of the siege of Troy. There were earlier great catastrophes which had plunged humanity backward for extended periods.

The practical implication for today is that we appear presently committed to plunging civilization into one of the worst and most prolonged such dark ages ever.[16]

Respecting the Vedic and classical Sanskrit literature itself, we have no doubt that the overthrow of the evil Harrapan culture was a happy accomplishment in net effect, but the Aryan invaders who accomplished

---

16. Marilyn Ferguson's **Aquarian Conspiracy** [Los Angeles, 1980] is to be taken seriously, not only as efficiently representing the policies of the Palo Alto circles around Stanford's Willis Harman, but also the networks associated historically with Bertrand Russell, Robert Hutchins, Aldous Huxley, and the Pugwash Conference and Club of Rome crowds generally: the countercultural "post-industrial" world-federalist utopianism.

this had undergone devastating cultural shocks prior to their arrival in the subcontinent. We know of two distinct such catastrophes. The first is emphasized by Tilak: the producers of the polar astronomical calendars had been driven by glaciation from their Arctic home. Then the Indo-European stock appears to have settled in central Asia during an extended period prior to the aridization of the region. This latter catastrophe had projected the Indo-European migrations into Europe and southern Asia during and after the third millennium B.C., gradually overwhelming and almost eradicating the remnants of an Atlas-culture dominating Western Europe, and becoming the Greeks, the Hittites, the Celts, and so forth.

Nonetheless the progress accomplished apart from the effects of such catastrophes is clear enough for our purposes.

The grand program for philology stipulated by Wilhelm von Humboldt bears directly on the issues here. Humboldt's work in philology proposed that first an Indo-European philology be developed, to define the philology of a common root-language. Using the experience so gained, philology must compare Indo-European language-species with Semite species, with Chinese species, and so forth. There are indications that many of these language-species have a common root, emphatically those associated with central Asian origins. Dr. Parpart noted recently the work of a scholar in Japan, who has documented evidence that modern Thai is a direct offshoot of the dominant language of ancient China. He concentrates on the musical inflections used, and suggests that modern Chinese has lost some of the inflection still preserved in Thai. In this respect, classical Greek, classical Sanskrit, Thai, Chinese, etc., have notable kinships. If we reconstruct a musical form of Indo-European, then the indicated comparison can be pursued accordingly.

The central question here is to what degree are the most advanced cultural features of ancient Indo-European, Chinese, etc. language-cultures common among such cultures by way of "lateral transmission," or "duplication of discovery," or attributable to a generating feature of some common language-culture? If the time span indicated by the Gulf-Stream version of Tilak's thesis is to be the basis for our reckoning, the case for importance of a common language-culture-origin is very strong.

Whatever further investigation proves on such points, such a working-hypothesis aids us by pushing our inquiries in the most fruitful directions. The universe is a stubborn critter: to obtain the right answer from it, you must first ask it the right question.

Standing back from the specifics of each period and place in the sweep of history [and pre-history], we ought to be astonished, at first thought, that two facts persist among all of the instances to be considered. First, that there are only three rigorously distinguishable moral types of individual personality and culture, corresponding to the "Inferno," "Purgatory," and "Paradise" of Dante Alighieri's **Commedia**.[17] Second, that these three moral types correspond to the primary combinations possible of two, opposing principles [e.g., republican versus oligarchical].

The latter two, opposing principles are implicitly the divine spark of creative-mental potential within each human individual, opposed to the bestial impulse ["original sin"] of irrationalistic hedonism ["anarchism," "existentialism"] also embedded in that same individual.

In the instance of the maturation of the individual within the setting of a moral form of society or culture, loving instruction of the anarchistic infant by the parents and others, nurtures the divine spark within the infant and child. By loving always only that in the infant and child which corresponds to the development and exercise of the divine spark, the new individual is encouraged to adopt the identity of a lovable personality accordingly. Maturation acquires thus the form of the new individual's inner struggle between the growing power of the divine spark and the opposing, bestial, impulses of anarchistic hedonism.[18] This is accomplished most effectively by avoiding what Riesman et al. might prefer to describe as merely an "other-directed" shaping of the social-identity preferences of the new individual; the child must not "be good" merely because this prompts favorable responses by parents and others. The child must discover that the good aspect of his or her nature is also an efficient power in the universe, the power of creative discovery. Of this, the child might say: "I can prove it for myself," or express the same point of view in asking the question "why, Daddy?"

If Daddy replies to the child's "Why?," with the ir-

---

17. Most notably, these three types are discussed under the heading of "Phoenician myths," by Socrates, in Plato's **Republic**. The same matter is treated by St. Augustine.

18. Adam Smith's "Invisible Hand," and Jeremy Bentham's hedonistic principle of his and John Stuart Mill's felicific calculus (utilitarianism), are examples of advocacy of immorality.

rationalist's: "Because your mother told you to do it," the child is being degraded thus into a cultural outlook of the "irrationalist-noun" variety. Better reply by Daddy would be either, "Come, I'll try to show you why," or, if the matter is beyond the child's reach, "When you're a little older, you'll be able to work this out for yourself."

If a child, asked what the child wishes to become in adulthood, replies, "I'm going to be...." ask that child "Why?" the child replies, in effect: "Then I'll be able to...," the implicit morality of the child's argument informs us of the probable direction of moral development occurring in that young person. If a child locates a sense of moral identity in the development of efficient powers of discovery, the processes of moral development are to that degree predominant, to that degree mastering the contrary, hedonistic impulses.

Friedrich Schiller

The same principles of development are also characteristic of cultures.

Immanual Kant reacted strongly against the immorality of David Hume.[19] What Kant denounced, with as much vehemence as Kant's public practice permitted him, was the immorality of that thesis of Hume's which forms the central principle of Hume, of Adam Smith, of Jeremy Bentham, and "nineteenth-century British philosophical radicalism." Hume, Smith, et al. argued that the imperfection of man's reason prevented the individual, or society, from precalculating the consequences of choices of behavior among the individual members of society, or by society as a whole. [Hence, Kant's charge of "philosophical indifferentism" against Hume.] This argument was employed by Hume, Smith, et al.[20] to propose that individual actions should be governed solely by "original and immediate instincts . . . of love of pleasure, and of dread of pain."[21]

As far as it went, Kant's extensive rebuttal against an empiricist morality was sound. The fallacies otherwise embedded in Kant's argument, already concomitants of the earlier **Critiques**, showed themselves at their worst in Kant's **Critique of Judgment** and his commentaries on aesthetics generally. It was on the latter point that Kant was most directly and efficiently corrected by the Friedrich Schiller Kant otherwise admired so much. Kant's essential argument on morality was presented in relatively most compact form in his **Critique of Practical Reason**.

Summarily, Kant argued that the "repression" of prohibited kinds of impulses and acts by society negated those hedonistic impulses within the individual. However, this "repression" was not merely a negation. Since this negation made the individual a social person, the negation corresponded to the individual's vital self-interest in establishing and maintaining a social identity. The desire for this social identity negated the negativity of "repression" [negation of the negation]; in this way, morality was described as made positive [by such "negation of the negation"].

Schiller corrected Kant on this point, showing that effective productions of the creative-mental potentials of the individual are a directly knowable form of the Good, and that, hence, morality need not be premised merely on the kind of double-negativity which Kant prescribed. Apart from this specific correction of Kant's views on aesthetics, the entirety of Schiller's later productions of drama are based on the principle he cited against Kant's error.

19. See I. Kant's **Prolegomena to Any Future Metaphysics,** and also his preface to the first edition of his **Critique of Pure Reason** [passim].
20. Adam Smith was a protégé of David Hume, and most directly influenced by Hume's **Treatise of Human Nature,** the chief reference-point for Smith's own 1759 **Theory of the Moral Sentiments**. The doctrine of the Invisible Hand is derived directly from the cited line of argument, in the **Wealth of Nations**.
21. Smith, **Theory of the Moral Sentiments,** as cited in LaRouche and Goldman, **The Ugly Truth About Milton Friedman** [New York, 1980] p. 107.

Commenting upon the Jacobin Terror in Paris, Schiller said famously: "the century has produced a great moment," referring to the trans-Atlantic movement led by Benjamin Franklin, "but," referring to the rise of the Jacobins in France, "the moment has found a little people." Using his resources as a leading historian of his time, Schiller composed a series of tragedies based on leading problems of statecraft in modern history of nations. Although Schiller employed some dramatic license, to deviate slightly from events as they had actually occurred in terms of individual personalities of the drama, the problems posed in each drama were true to-life insofar as the tragic events as a whole were concerned. The function of these dramas, as Schiller himself described in considerable detail in his writings or. his methods of composition, was to show to audiences that in the course of critical events the point is reached at which an available solution is clear, but in which influential figures and general populations each fail to act upon that solution; the failure to act so then traps the population in a tragic development which the population is thereafter unable to resist. These immensely popular dramas of Schiller have been proven to have been the single leading moral influence which later mobilized the German people to fight the successful Liberation War against Napoleon Bonaparte—a war led by such friends of Schiller's as Freiherr vom Stein and Wilhelm von Humboldt.

It is possible, in fact, as well as abstract scientific reflections, to mobilize a leading force of a people to foresee more or less accurately the outcome of the policy-actions of nations, and also the contributions to those actions by individuals. Although Kant was admitted to the inner elite of the circles around Schiller, Koerner, von Humboldt, et al., it was Schiller, not Kant, who made possible the defeat of Napoleon's tyranny—just as the 1815 Congress of Vienna, and Metterrnich's Prussian agent G.W.F. Hegel, launched an inquisition against the writings of Schiller, as well as against Schiller's friends, in the effort to reverse the republican achievements of 1809-1814 under vom Stein, Scharnhorst, Humboldt et al. The efficient power to uplift a people, morally, and in its general condition otherwise, is direct access to and service of the creative-mental principle.

Nonetheless, Kant's thesis of the **Critique of Practical Reason** is an exceptional insight into the mechanisms of mind as a resident of Dante's Purgatory. The resident of Purgatory, like Kant, adheres to morality

Joseph Karl Stieler

Wilhelm von Humboldt

with a sense of duty, and is always conscious of duty as in some sense an act of self-denial, an act of "repression" of his bestial, irrationalistic [anarchistic, existentialist] "original and immediate instincts." He is not a resident of Paradise, not one of Schiller's "Beautiful Souls"; yet, at worst, the resident of Purgatory is fortunately not a radical empiricist of the sort recommended by Hume, Smith, Bentham or John Stuart Mill, not a resident of the Inferno.

Even among the best modern republics, such as our own has been during its best periods, the development of our culture, and the maturation of individuals within that culture, has been defective to the degree that the moral strata of our electorates have been chiefly residents of Purgatory, not Beautiful Souls. This defect of even moral populations was a subject of special attention by Plato, notably in his **Republic**. He stipulated that the design of republics must therefore be such as to efficiently deal with such defects of maturation within the electorate generally. He argued, as Solon of Athens had argued the importance of writing out his constitutional poem to guide Athens thereafter, that a people must bind itself to a written body of constitutional law, and practice obedience to that law, rather than relying upon its own independent judgment; hence, in modern times, we speak of our republic as a government under law, rather than as a government by men. It were desirable that electorates be dominated by Beautiful Souls—residents of Dante's Paradise. Lacking thus far that circumstance, we must compensate for the defects in our own people by choosing republics premised upon constitutional law. For obvious reasons, Plato described this expedient arrangement as "the second-best form of republic."

It should be seen readily enough, that the philosophical outlook of the residents of Paradise is characteristically of the religious-cultural species we identified as "rational-verb," and Inferno's "irrationalist noun."

It is "human nature" that the moral impulses of the individual and cultures composed of individuals, are not more than two: the irrationalistic, hedonistic impulses which echo the "original and immediate instincts" of a beast, in opposition to the creative-mental potentials, the divine spark which distinguishes man from the beast. Hence, only two generative impulses are possible within individuals and cultures.

The behavior of the individual, under the conflicting influence of such two impulses, is always governed by what rigorous clinical psychology can distinguish in each instance as a controlling sense of personal social identity. Individual judgments are not premised on the individual's sense of biological identity, but of social identity subsuming biological identity. This choice of social identity regulates the person's definition of "self-interest." This sense of identity, and notion of self-interest, is defined primarily by which of the three types of moral identity (Inferno, Purgatory, Paradise) the individual has adopted. That is, the individual identifies either:

1. Completely with irrationalist hedonism ("original and immediate instincts"),

2. Completely with a "Kantian" sense of social identity (Purgatory), or

3. Creative-mental life (Paradise).

That choice of identity defines perceived self-interest. This sense of self-interest directs the exercise of judgment. Judgment so directed determines human activity, and also determines how the individual judges the results of his activity.

The first, the choice of the Inferno as the location in which one's identity (and self-interest) resides, is dominated by subordination of rationality to "original and immediate instincts," as Dante describes this so aptly. The second, the Kantian, might appear, at first glance, to have a dual identity, a conflict between morality and "original and immediate instincts." Yet, as Kant argues correctly to that degree, the resident of Purgatory locates his or her identity in the moral "sense of duty" to prohibit those actions of "original and immediate instincts," which are prohibited by the morality. The third, Paradise, prompts the individual to locate his or her identity, and self-interest, in that policy of self-development and practice which fosters predictably some durable benefit to present and future generations.

It might appear, to superficial observation, that the resident of Paradise and Purgatory eat and clothe themselves in similar manner. Yet, the resident of Paradise views these matters quite differently than does the Kantian. "I require that which affords me the power to contribute to present and future generations": For the Kantian, the end-result of the morally permitted form of sensuous individual experience is the individual pleasure or other individual benefit of the individual in himself. For the resident of Paradise, the individual benefit of such sensuous experience is limited to its universal consequences, the contribution of that individual sensuous experience to the individual's power to accomplish some necessary good for present and future generations. The sense of self-interest embodied in the individual action is different. Such a distinction may appear almost indiscernible in an isolated action of this sort; it becomes clearly discernible when we compare the general policies of ordering of personal life between Beautiful Souls and Kantians. The Beautiful Soul subordinates what might be defined as a Kantian sort of self-interest to a higher purpose, a universal purpose. Imagine Friedrich Schiller eating and drinking his favorite wine during the periods his life was dedicated to fashioning tragedies intended to uplift the German people to a state they would not repeat those errors of France through which the Jacobins came to power; that is the eating and drinking of a Beautiful Soul.

Only two kinds of opposing impulses exist within individual persons; the bestial impulses of irrationalist "original and immediate instincts," opposing the sense of beauty in efficiently developing and exercising creative-mental potentials in service of universal good. These two, opposing impulses permit only three categorical kinds of personal identity to occur within individuals and cultures. We witness only two opposing forces in the making of all human history and pre-history, and we witness only three categorical cultural types emerging in this sweep of human existence as a whole. We witness such because nothing else were possible. Clearly, the following table of comparisons follows:

Identity	Cultural Matrix	Religion Type
Inferno	irrationalist-noun	SHAKTI-ISHTAR
Purgatory	rational-noun	GOD IS KING
Paradise	rational-verb	APOSTOLIC CHRISTIANITY

This summary table is adequate to guide us in interpreting those characteristics of cultures bearing upon the potential of those cultures to foster and assimilate fundamental scientific discovery.

The ascent from baboon-like gathering-cultures toward civilization is implicitly inevitable, since the divine spark of creative-mental potential is that which absolutely, categorically distinguishes mankind from baboons. It were worse than absurd to attempt to adduce the "evolutionary development" of human characteristics from the great apes, as if by aid of Boltzmann's LaPlaceian theory of fluctuations. Human development depends upon a quality categorically absent from the great apes, some feature of the human organization corresponding to the human soul, congruent with the verb "to think creatively." This is the characteristic of human cultures, which distinguishes "human ecology" absolutely, categorically from "animal ecology." To attempt to apply "animal ecology" to mankind is an absurdity in principle, as absurd as applying the "ecology" of "societies of rocks" to the biosphere generally. The possibility of Paradise is implicit in the human soul; that is not only a theological doctrine, but the one empirical fact about human existence which is absolutely incontestable, man's increase of his species' potential relative population-density through technological progress.

From that standpoint, it is not astonishing that a pre-Vedic culture could have developed an astronomy far more advanced in quality than that of cultures of the Mesopotamian series.

The problem to be considered is not how mankind could have developed a stunningly beautiful advance in astronomy so early. The problem to be considered is, mankind having achieved such a level of culture, how were it possible culture could degenerate to such levels as the Mesopotamian series?

The answer is before our eyes, both in John Dewey's programs for public education, and in the more radical version of such policies promoted by the National Education Association today. The essence of the practice, in both of these abominations, is asserting the "freedom" of the child's impulses at the expense of developing rigorous knowledge in the child and adolescent. "Permissive child-rearing" is of the same species of morally destructive policies. It is chiefly through the impact of such morally degraded school room and family policies upon several successive generations of our population, that we as a nation have been brought into a moral condition increasingly approximating that of the Biblical Sodom and Gomorrah. In brief, such policies intervene against the development of the child, to promote the interest of bestial "original and immediate instincts."

The conditions of life, most emphatically the low life-expectancies of gathering-societies, are obviously a great impediment to unleashing of the divine spark within the individual. Lacking a more rigorously defined set of parameters, it is fair to use our rough estimate, that the life-expectancy of a primitive gathering-culture must be significantly below twenty years of age. It would be useful to produce a study of the estimated demographic characteristics of such a culture: life-expectancy of surviving infants, rates of infant mortality, differential rates of mortality among males and females, and among males for all reasons as compared with females for reasons other than childbearing. Lacking such clearly feasible studies, it is fair to estimate that females would predominate in the adult segment of the population, and that the majority of the population would be composed of pre-adolescent individuals.

In such circumstances, the cult of the mother-goddess and "matriarchical society" are most probable features of culture. The predominance of children still dominated by strong maternal dependency—e.g., relative infantilism of character-formation—means that the infantile (hedonistic-irrationalist) element must tend to be the characteristic of such cultures. This is no conjecture: the characteristics of all Whore-of-Babylon forms of religious-cultural matrices conform precisely to features adduced from the case of such a primitive and degenerate form of "matriarchical" society. The ambiguity, in such cases as Shakti-Siva, or Isis-Osiris, whether Siva-Osiris is simply the consort or the incestuous son of the mother-goddess is consistent with that connection to primitive gathering-societies. In both instances, Siva and Osiris, the male phallic figure is clearly the subordinate figure; the Cybele-Dionysos connection is exemplary, as is the equivalence of Siva Osiris-Satan-Dionysos: nasty characters all. The addition of the Horus-Lucifer-Apollo figure reeks of primitive, incest-ridden societies of the most abominable ethics. Perhaps the National Educational Association would be pleased by such past outcomes of the policies it presently promotes. Sodom and Gomorrah, and the use of the name "sodomy," implies the general results to which NEA policies must tend to lead.

wikimedia commons

The Congress of Vienna.

We find a relevant case in the process leading into the emergence of Nazism in Germany. Generally, the Conservative Revolution of former Waffen-SS volunteer, Dr. Armin Mohler of the Siemens Stiftung, describes the process with about as much accuracy as one could expect from a hard-core philosophical Nazi. It was the "romantic movement" in Germany, promoted so energetically in the boudoir of Switzerland's Madame de Staël, which is the philosophical root of Nazism in Germany historically. However, Mohler leaves out of account certain of the crucial circumstances.

As Helga Zepp-LaRouche has documented in several locations,[22] perhaps the highest point of development in European culture was reached during the upsurge of the German nation in support of the Liberation War against Bonaparte's tyranny. Everything which Leibniz, Franklin, and others had worked to set into motion was rallied in Germany around the circles of collaborators of Schiller and Freiherr vom Stein. Such giants of music as Wolfgang Mozart and Ludwig von Beethoven were integral parts of the same Franklin-linked trans-Atlantic conspiracy as Schiller, von Cotta,

et al. The joy, the cultural optimism in Germany, from the onset of the Liberation Wars, until the eve of the 1815 Congress of Vienna, is without known precedent in modern European history. The superiority of German classical culture—in music, poetry, drama: the "nation of poets and thinkers"—from that period, has been justly, variously envied, emulated, and celebrated in the literature and concert-halls of the civilized world since. Upon these same foundations, the recognized world-superiority of German science and advances in technology, through World War I, was established. How could a people who had once so excelled degenerate into Nazism?

It began, as Helga Zepp-LaRouche emphasizes with the Congress of Vienna itself. The Venetian nobleman, Count Capodistria, which Venice had imposed upon Czar Alexander I as Russia's foreign minister, employed his tools, Clement Prince Metternich and the notoriously odious Talleyrand, to impose the nightmare of the Holy Alliance upon continental Europe. Whether through corruption, simple meanness of character, or folly of weak-mindedness, the ruling Hohenzollern of Prussia betrayed all those around Freiherr vom Stein who had just earlier saved Prussia and the Hohenzollern throne from Napoleon's destruction. That monarch betrayed the entire German people, and so the overwhelming majority of those people regarded the development. Soon, Schiller's and Humboldt's ad-

---

22. A forthcoming book, including her introduction, will supply a freshly documented overview of the Nazi phenomenon to German readers.

versary, the Metternich agent, Professor G.W.F. Hegel, became Prussia's "state philosopher." For a time, Schiller's writings were virtually banned from Prussia! In betrayal and frustration, Germany sank into despair, into the cultural pessimism which made possible the recruiting of the children of the pre-1815 German republicans to Guisseppe Mazzini's 1848-1849 radical upsurge [e.g. Karl Marx].

With the later rise of Bismarck, the oligarchical forces behind the dissolved Holy Alliance strengthened their grip on Germany. By the beginning of the 1890s, the forerunners of Nazism were already afoot in circles including that of Chamberlain, Neitzsche, and Bakunin's old Young Germany crony, Richard Wagner. The World War, the masses of "rootless ones" of a lost generation of soldiers returned from the fronts, and the destruction of institutions and hope under the terms of Versailles, crystallized the successive moral defeats of the post 1814 period into the dionysian orgy of Nazism.

Notably, the cultural matrix chiefly referenced for creating Nazism in Germany was Russian culture. "Solidarism," which produced Gregor Strasser and Josef Goebbels, was explicitly a Russian import of "Tolstoyian" ideology. "Third Reich" was a name contributed to Nazi dogma by Dostoevsky's influential Berlin publicist, Moeller van den Bruck; the model for this was Dostoevsky's demand for a "Third Rome"—a pan-slavic world empire with Moscow as its capital. The Nazi's chief "philosopher," Alfred Rosenberg, who completed his education in Bolshevik Moscow before arriving in Bavaria, was another leading Russophile among Nazi ideologues. Germany lacked the elaborated "counterculture" to meet Houston Chamberlain's, Nietzsche's, Rosenberg's, and Hitler's requirement that the last vestiges of Judeo-Christian civilization be uprooted from Germany: the "blood and soil" cults typical of Russian culture were therefore imported as the model of reference for creating "Nazi culture." The difference between the Russian Dostoevskyans and the Nazis was the issue of which "race" would prevail in establishing the "Third Rome" [Third Reich] which had been the impassioned aspiration of Russian culture since the second coronation of Ivan the Terrible. [So, in 1941, it was the Nazi legions of the Russian Raskol'nik, Dostoevsky, which butchered invaded Russia in the manner of Russian berzerkers; and, it was Dostoevsky's Russian Raskol'niki who struck back with a berzerker's axe-wielding fervor of murder and rape indigenous to the Russian variety of this cultural strain—as Ilya Ehrenberg's war-time propaganda from Moscow luridly attests.]

The account of the Atlas people in Didorus Siculus's account can not be put aside as merely a legend. The corroborating evidence, both internal and circumstantial, is too abundant. A maritime culture's colony was established near the Straits of Gibraltar. The indigenous people were a brutish gathering-society culture, to whom the urban maritime colonists introduced agriculture. Intermarriage occurred, according to the account. The children of a concubine revolted and took power in a bloody, three-way coup d'état. The victors of that coup d'état, led by the son of the concubine, Zeus, constitute the kernel of the Hesiodic pantheon, the Norse gods, and so forth.

This intersects events which Plato attributes to about 10,000 B.C. or earlier, a dating which agrees with as much evidence as we have on the latest antiquity for existence of a maritime culture of the type described in the Didorus Siculus account.

If a culture permeated with the Shakti-Ishtar religious-cultural matrix assimilated the technology produced by a more advanced culture, that appropriation of technology provides the kind of picture exhibited by the morally degenerated cultures characteristic of the Mesopotamian series. The troublesome point here is that we might tend to assume that the assimilation of advanced technology should foster improvement in the religious-cultural matrix in such a case. The solution for the apparent paradox so posed is obtained readily, by recognizing that cultures as a whole are governed by a controlling sense of identity, in a sense coherent with the control of individual behavior by a categorical type of social identity. In the cases that two opposing cultures are blended, the outcome is determined by which of those cultures supplies the sense of identity for the leading institutions of the combined culture.

In the instance of a "blood and soil" culture, the "racialist" element is axiomatic. A "Whore of Babylon" culture defines itself in terms of a particular group of people associated with the "blood and soil." This is consistent with the kind of infantile matrix of such religious-cultural currents' connections of "matriarchical" primitive cultures. The "blood and soil" feature is not something added to the Shakti-Ishtar matrix, but a coherent feature of the principled elements earlier identified.

Compare the recent centuries' history of the United

States, France, and Germany (for example). Up to World War I, these nations' populations were a composite of numerous immigrant strata, each of which became more or less "American," "French," or "German," respectively at fairly rapid rates. The relatively more advanced the cultural level of any particular group of immigrants, in each case, and the more rapidly it reached economic parity with the nation's population generally, the more rapidly it was assimilated. Conversely, strata immigrating from very poor foreign populations, with low levels of literacy, and who progressed slowly in assimilating economically, the rate of assimilation was relatively slower. Apart from embedded racial or ethnic prejudices, the populations of these nations are relatively the least racialist in the entire history of culture known to us.

wikipedia
Augustine of Hippo (354–430 CE) as painted by Botticelli.

This happy feature of our national cultures (at least, relatively speaking) is a peculiarity of Western Christendom. Those of us typical of this cultural heritage are often astonished to think of a fellow-citizen as being of a different race, or different ethnic origin otherwise. It is the character, the mind of the person which interests us, and which is usually the leading premise of all our practical judgments respecting that person. Our national consciences tend to be offended, ashamed, when we are confronted with prejudices, especially injustices, linked to some biological distinction in the race or national origin of another person. We err, however, whenever we of this cultural heritage of St. Augustine project such happy norms upon the presumed behavior of other cultures. We find it difficult to reconstruct in our own minds that special sort of world-outlook which demands a bloody vendetta against all people of some differing religious affiliation or racial or national-origin characteristics. It is sometimes difficult for us to regard as more than an unfortunate, temporary aberration the explosion of some degraded outburst as: "1 don't care about the rest of the world; I care only about my race!" We find it difficult to believe that vast extent of cultures on this planet, still today, not only believe that, but have that prejudice embedded in them as a primary motivation.

We fail to grasp what a revolutionary change it was, that St. Paul undertook in his mission to the Gentiles, bearing the message of the opening verses of the Gospel of St. John. Neither Plato nor Socrates would have disagreed with Paul's policy, but Plato's work lacked that specific genius which the Jesus Christ of St. John's Gospel afforded humanity. That a religion, Christian Judaism, should not limit its mission to the Jews, but should embrace all mankind as brothers, was, as New Testament theology insists, a New Dispensation in the ordering of mankind's affairs. Perhaps, long, long ago, in a time before Wilhelm von Humboldt's version of the Tower of Babel occurred, such a notion of the unity of mankind existed among some common forebears of Indo-European and Chinese culture, for example. If so, it was later lost, and lost for a very, very long time. Only with the opening passages of John's Gospel and the mission of Paul to the Gentiles, did at least part of humanity regain that which may have been lost long before. Let us not propose here to meddle in the religious affairs of peoples, but, otherwise, the realization of that moral unity of mankind expressed by Paul's mission is long overdue for this planet of ours.

The idea that culture is "racial" in character, the characteristic feature of the Babylonian and Persian empires, for example, is key to the way in which a degraded sort of religious-cultural matrix resists the moralizing benefits of a superior culture whose achievements it has acquired in one fashion or another.

It is not only true, but rather fundamentally so, that a policy of practice directed toward scientific-technological progress fosters moral development in the culture and population so affected. Yet, the presence or absence of technological advancement does not occur within the setting of a cultural tabula rasa. Moral uplifting must fight against both endemic and institutionalized bestiality, not only against the endemic "original sin" of "original and immediate instincts," but also against hegemonic cultural institutions whose characteristic sense of identity is anti-progress. Scientific-technological progress is a force for moral advancement, but it is a force which must acquire allies within a society if it is to shape the moral policy of practice of that society as a whole. Sometimes, it is necessary that the leading institutions of a nation be destroyed, that mankind might be rid of a degenerate variety of culture. Too often, nothing exists to destroy the grip of an evil culture upon a people but its own internal, self-induced collapse—like the self-induced collapse of the evil Roman culture in Italy. There is, as Schiller defines this a *punctum saliens* in the course of a nation's or culture's slide into doom, a jumping-off point at which the enactment of some available, specific sort of change of policy-direction in practice might nullify the slide toward self-destruction; up to that point, a people gripped by a decaying culture might still be rescued by their own resources. If the opportunity of the *punctum saliens* is missed, thereafter there is nothing that a people might attempt by its own independent means to prevent the remorseless unfolding of the tragedy. Tacitus' account of Rome under the immediate successors of Augustus Caesar is a vivid portrait of a culture so degenerate it could no longer be saved by efforts from within itself.

As we indicated the feasibility of estimating the demographic characteristics of a brutish matriarchical form of society, reasonable estimates could be constructed for a maritime culture of the sort indicated. The qualitatively more favorable demography of an emergent maritime culture, relative to an inland gathering-culture, may not in itself cause the kind of moral development leading into the results demonstrated by ancient astronomical calendars, but without such qualitative advantage such a moral development were unlikely. What is also certain is that the transition from fishing at mouths of notable rivers to a maritime culture of the development indicated by the calendars subsumes certain rigorously definable technological revolutions, to the effect: A culture which has produced such calendars has overcome the challenge of those technological revolutions required to progress from a rudimentary fishing-culture.

For example: the transition from fishing by landing, wading or near-shore swimming to the first approximations of use of navigable rafts and boats. For example: open-water navigation, especially such navigation at night-time. For example: the discovery of the sidereal year, the solar year, the progress of the equinox, and so forth.

We must distinguish the process of "original" discovery in such cultures from the "lateral" adoption of a technology by a culture which does not experience in its religious-cultural matrix the capabilities of having effected such a technological discovery.

It is sometimes unavoidable, as a matter of practice, that developing nations today be supplied with 'turn-key" technology. Yet, to sustain self-generating technological progress within a developing nation, the nation must develop scientific and capital-goods, producing institutions at international "state of the art" levels of development: not necessarily the full range of all "state of the art" technologies, but of some such technologies, and to the effect that those mastered are representative of the principles subsuming more or less all "state of the art" science and technology. The practical comprehension of "state of the art" science and technology must become embedded within the cultural matrix of the nation.

In the instance of the development of the maritime culture which generated the indicated early astronomical calendars, it was necessary that the indicated sort of steps of technological revolutions be embedded as experience in the cultural matrix: that an effect congruent with the hypothesis of the higher hypothesis, such a principle of discovery.

Imagine yourself a small population of some urban site of such a maritime culture. With aid of the minimum essential megalithic structures, determine the sidereal year, and the progression of the equinox. Expanding the megalithic observatory appropriately, extend the astronomy in the direction indicated by the fragmentary astronomical calendars under consideration here.

What are the characteristics of, and preconditions for the development of such calendars in this way?

Broadly, the principles of synthetic geometry are implicit in the effort. Only the circle, the sphere are self-evident existences. Existence is otherwise a transitive verb, defined in respect to circular rotation. Rotation (cycle) must be correlated with rotation, and all correlated with a single, fundamental rotation.

EDITORIAL

In the Stars, The Long Awaited Age of Reason

*There, in the stars, lies the long awaited Age of Reason, when
our species sheds at last the cultural residue of the beast.*
—Lyndon LaRouche

by Kesha Rogers

April 24—In less than three weeks, the most critical international conference in the period since World War II—the Beijing Belt and Road summit—will convene. On May 14 and 15, the leaders and heads of state of 28 nations will gather, joined by representatives of 110 countries, industry leaders, business leaders, and others. It has already been announced that Russia's President Putin will be the first guest of honor at the conference.

During the last three years, an invitation has been repeatedly extended to the United States to take up the offer of Chinese President Xi Jinping for win-win cooperation, to join in the great economic development perspective of the Belt and Road, for the benefit of all nations involved. This offer was first made to former President Obama in 2014, but was summarily rejected by the British-run Wall Street stooge who was then occupying the White House. Obama chose geopolitical confrontation over working with China and other nations for the good of mankind.

Now a new opportunity has presented itself. President Trump has expressed serious interest in, and has already taken initial steps toward developing a friendly working relationship with China, as was demonstrated in his recent discussions with President Xi at Mar-a-Lago, Florida. Again, the offer of "win-win" peaceful cooperation has been put forth, this time to President Trump. The opportunity now before the United States is very real. Were America to seize this opportunity, the murderous banking and financial looting policies of London and Wall Street might be replaced with a future of expanded economic opportunity, peace, and scientific progress. Those are the implications of accepting China's offer to join in a commitment to the common aims of mankind through win-win cooperation. If President Trump were to announce his intention to attend the Belt and Road conference in May, this alone would be a singular action that could well shift the entire global picture.

Not least in importance, greater collaboration with the nations of the Belt and Road will give great impetus and greatly enhanced potential for joint efforts in science, particularly cooperative work toward the exploration and development of space. With full U.S. participation, a leap for all of mankind in space exploration becomes immediately and rapidly possible.

The Optimism of Space

On Monday, April 24, President Trump spoke with astronauts on the International Space Station (ISS). He was joined in the Oval Office by his daughter Ivanka and astronaut Kate Rubins, and together they spoke with NASA ISS Commander Peggy Whitson and Col. Jack Fischer. The dialogue between the ISS astronauts and the President was broadcast live into hundreds of classrooms and space facilities around the United States, and was streamed and viewed worldwide as well.

The President honored Commander Whitson for her achievements as the first female commander of the ISS and for having spent more time in space than any other American astronaut. Their discussion touched on several topics, including a report from Whitson on the need to understand how microgravity works in space and how it effects the human body. She also reported that ISS astronauts are studying the problems of long-duration space missions, and the technological advances that will be required. More than 200 scientific experiments are currently underway aboard the space station.

Col. Fischer stressed the critical importance of international cooperation in space exploration. He talked about his trip to the ISS aboard the Soyuz with his Russian counterpart, veteran Cosmonaut Fyodor Yurchikhin. Col. Fischer said, "The international space station is, by far, the best example of international cooperation and what we can do when we work together, in the history of humanity."

Both American astronauts were explicit about the optimism and inspiration that participation in this mission has given them. This was demonstrated most beautifully by Col. Fischer, when he said, "I would say to all the students that are watching, the time to get excited is now. If you aren't studying science and math, you might want to think about that, because our future in the stars starts now, and you can be a part of that, if, like Dr. Whitson, you can find that passion and work really hard. And we're going to find a permanent foothold in the stars for humanity if you do that."

The Role of the Visionary

On March 25, the Schiller Institute held an extraordinary conference in Berlin, Germany, to honor the one hundredth anniversary of the birth of the great space pioneer Krafft Ehricke. Under the banner of "Krafft Ehricke's Vision for the Future of Mankind," Ehricke's prime thesis that there are no limitations to the progress of mankind in the Universe was celebrated and discussed. As if a divine hand had intervened, on the very day of that conference, President Trump gave his truly inspiring national address, in which he declared, after signing the NASA Authorization Act, "With this legislation, we renew our national commitment to NASA's mission of exploration and discovery. And we continue a tradition that is as old as mankind. We look to the heavens with wonder and curiosity."

If we are to take up this challenge today, it is of paramount importance that every American fully grasp the critical importance of this effort on behalf of all mankind, for the necessary future of all. It must also be a shared commitment. All nations—all of humanity—must benefit from the cooperation among nations for the peaceful use and development of outer space. This is the ultimate win-win solution for all nations. It can be realized through crash programs, what Lyndon La-Rouche has described as "the tight integration of the most advanced, most fundamental scientific research with the production and development of new technologies in a general way, such that there is no organizational separation between the most fundamental scientific research and production in general."

The Time to Act Is Now

Many initiatives are already underway. On April 22, China celebrated its second annual national space day by carrying out the docking of the Tianzhou 1 supply ship with China's Tianzhou 2 space lab, 240 miles above the Earth. Two days later—the same day that President Trump spoke with the ISS astronauts—China celebrated the anniversary of China's first space satellite, launched on April 24, 1970.

Full participation by the United States in the upcoming Beijing Belt and Road Summit would have the immediate effect of advancing this progress dramatically. This is just what is needed. A new future beckons, one in which the legacy of war, zero growth, and cultural decay will become a memory. Bold action now will make the difference for future generations.